Prospero Books

presents

PLEASE BUY THIS BOOK

PLEASE BUY THIS BOOK!

Gift Books For Good Causes 1898 to 1945

by
James Havers

'Belgium' by W H Caffyn – *The Blinded Soldiers and Sailors Gift Book*

CONTENTS

AN INTRODUCTION

'Bless My soul!' by Lewis Baumer – *Princess Mary's Gift Book*

Why, you may wonder, have they been so overlooked?

A century ago, these lovely books graced many homes. For the most part they were beautiful, drafted by the finest writers and highly-regarded artists, full of first-hand personal insights into our history, and are still not hard to find. Nor are they expensive.

How could this be?

Today we live in an over-supplied age – those of us in the developed world, that is. Every day we are bombarded with exhortations to buy – from shop windows as we pass, from magazines and newspapers, from the internet – and because we live in a successful consumerist society we accumulate. We gather clutter. We buy so much food we throw much of it away. We have so many records bought or downloaded to our collections that, if we were to sit down and play every one of them just once, it might take a year. Some we may never play again. Yet we keep them. We always did, and now they can be stored on a single hard disk, memory stick, phone or Cloud we luxuriate in the fact that we need never throw a single one away.

Those of us who love books – real ink-and-paper physical books – have bookcases filled with titles that we have read, titles we have never read but will not part with, and others that we intend to read sometime. As perhaps we will, one day. Now that books have followed records down the digital route they can be amassed and kept . . . and kept. We have been encouraged to look upon books as low-cost, low maintenance consumables: books are everywhere, in the supermarket, on your phone or your PC. You can have any book you like. You deserve it. Buy today.

Read tomorrow, if at all.

It hasn't always been this way. Two hundred years ago books were scarce. By *one* hundred years ago they'd become commonplace, and many of them *looked* commonplace – they were, after all, just for reading. The ordinary reader then, spending a few shillings on a novel, was aware of other more beautiful and considerably more expensive books, but didn't buy them; they were luxury items, too expensive. Those books, the equivalents of today's high-quality coffee-table books, were to be displayed or given as gifts – but if you were on an ordinary income, as most people were, you had to ignore such horribly expensive books; they weren't for you.   Only if you were better off or someone's birthday loomed, might you splash out. You might buy a gift book.

A century or so ago such books were lovely. Among many beautifully illustrated titles came *Arthur Rackham's Book of Pictures*, his *Aesop*, his *Peter Pan; Edmund Dulac's Fairy Book*, Charles Robinson's *Big Book of Fables* or *The Child's Christmas*, Florence Harrison's *Elfin Song* and Charles Folkard's *Pinocchio* or *Mother Goose*.

Who wouldn't want to own such things? Perhaps, occasionally, you might have bought one of the less expensive gift books – for a favourite grandchild, perhaps, as a birthday or Christmas present, but generally you thought you couldn't afford such things at all. Even though you wanted one. You would love to have owned such a thing. This has always been the way the market works: there is always something that costs more than you feel you can afford. (Today's billionaire buys a Lear jet or sumptuous mansion, then finds he has only reached the entry level to that exclusive market; there is always a better product, and there is always the urge to own more than one.)

What if . . . What if one of these splendid items were to come within your reach? What if one of them, without loss of quality, were to be mass-produced, and thus affordable? What if – and here comes the perfect justification – the money you paid for that beautiful item were to go to charity? How could you resist? Why should you?

You, the intelligent consumer of a hundred years ago, would have been up to the minute enough to know that new products and improvements appear on the market first at a high price and in small quantity until, as quantity increases, the price reduces and suddenly they become available to all. The first automobile was for the gentry, but by the middle of the 20th century it was the ambition of every family. By the century's close it had become everyday. When pocket calculators were first introduced in the 1970s they astounded the world, made people envious, yet within a decade their price fell from several hundred pounds apiece to being practically given away. Today's electronics follow a familiar path as the gadgets glide from being things we wish we could own to things we cannot do without. So it has been with books.

From papyri to codex, from illuminated manuscripts to print, from short print-runs to mass edition, the price kept falling. Print quality improved, and illustration became almost commonplace, moving in the 19th century from steel and copper engravings to wood engravings, from wood to photo-mechanical – and in the same way that today's move from paper-based books to electronic has brought prices tumbling down, so did they fall in the 19th century. Books came from the presses faster, cheaper and seemingly better than ever before. Illustration – once a rarity – became increasingly common, especially for books that were intended as possessions, books to be looked at and admired.

A typical frontispiece from the 1830s

In those days (some 30 years from around 1820 to the 1850s) the Gift Book market largely comprised elegant, if fairly dull, teatime books such as *Friendship's Offering, The Bijou, The Keepsake* and *The Drawing Room Scrapbook.* Copper and steel engraving had ruled supreme, but then came the revised, improved craft of wood engraving, with pictures finely *engraved* across the hardwood grain rather than *cut* crudely along it (as in wood*cuts*). Wood engravings, unlike metal, could be set into type and printed in the same run as the text, saving money and allowing more variety of design onto the

11

page. For the customer, once again, it meant a better product at a lower price.

The years that followed, an extended decade around the 1860s, have long been regarded as a golden age for illustrated books. Although the pictures were mainly in black and white, they were often fashioned by top artists. It was from wood engravings that the bold new Pre-Raphaelites earned bread and butter money, as did well-known genre, landscape and portrait artists. Their fine pictures graced table books, children's books and magazines.

Books had become big business. Where a hundred years before they had been the prerogative of individual booksellers they were now the valuable property of large firms. At the top end of the market, in terms of quality if not necessarily of profit, were lavish picture books: picture albums, annuals, art books, children's books and gift books. Many of these were beautiful, desirable then and still collectable today.

The term Gift Book covers a wide field, from exquisite productions made in tiny numbers by private presses, through to expensive trade editions or, at the opposite end of the scale, mass-market picture books. It is in a combination of these categories, the expensive and the mass-market picture book, that we find the subject of this study: the Gift Book Sold For Charity. Here the advantages of mass-production could be writ large. Some of these volumes reused plates for pictures used in previous, more expensive, books but with the lower costs of mass-production it was possible to commission fresh illustrations (bulked up, perhaps, with work from less expensive artists). Reprinted pictures, And even at times reprinted words, brought costs right down.

But the quality stayed high. Consider, as an early example of the Gift Book Sold For Charity, *The Queen's*

Christmas Carol. It came, as the title suggests, under the imprimatur of no less a personage than the Queen – King Edward VII's Queen Alexandra, a famous beauty in her day (though her day had been decades earlier) and a woman noted for her charitable works. The book was issued in 1905 in aid of her **Royal Fund for the Unemployed**. It looked good, the cause was good – how could any decent-minded citizen refuse?

1902. Alexandra Coronation day

Three years later came another Christmas Gift Book from the Queen. This one was different; instead of presenting contributions from famous authors and artists the book purported to have been compiled directly by the Queen herself. *Queen Alexandra's Christmas Gift Book* was a facsimile of what appeared to be her own private snapshot album, with loose informal photographs tipped in, several to a page – an album similar to one you might have of your own family at home!

Edward of Wales (1904)

A public appetite had been whetted – an appetite for beautiful-looking books produced in high numbers and sold at prices ordinary buyers could afford. *The Queen's Christmas Carol* had aped the style and borrowed artwork and plates from more expensive Gift Books, showing that it was possible for books that looked as if they belonged in upper-middle-class drawing rooms or libraries to be displayed in domestic parlours and enjoyed in more humble homes.

The heyday for Gift Books was approaching, and that heyday was the First World War. Within weeks of war's commencement, Belgium was invaded. Then Belgium fell. Publishers scrambled to be the first with war-time Gift Books – and made a surprisingly good job of them. On behalf of Gallant Belgium came *King Albert's Book* (King Albert being the king of fallen Belgium). It sold in large numbers, and is the Gift Book most commonly found in second-hand bookshops today. An Australian equivalent (comprising mainly Australian artists) came in 1915 with *Melba's Gift Book* (Nellie Melba being Australia's greatest opera singer; Peach Melba was named after her). This book, too, appealed on behalf of Belgium. A specifically British appeal (the **National Relief Fund**) was supported with *Princess Mary's Gift Book*. Money for wounded soldiers and sailors was raised with *The Queen's Gift Book* and in the same year, 1915, with *The Blinded Soldiers and Sailors Gift Book*.

Gift Books continued after the war for different causes and, some would say, with a drop in quality. The Prince of Wales was swift off the mark, issuing a fairly uninteresting book of photographs, *A Pictorial Record of the Voyages of HMS "Renown" 1919-1920*, on behalf of **St Dunstan's Hospital**. 1924 saw the *British Legion Album* which, though finely produced, was only a paperback (albeit larger than practically any other paperback), and production standards dropped again with the interwar *Legion Book* of 1929, which contained no tipped-in colour plates and no facsimile signatures. Those lovely tipped-in plates would not return. By the 1930s, readers had become more sophisticated, less likely to gasp at lavishly produced coffee-table books. People had become blasé, less likely to show off the books they owned; books were plentiful and people were less likely to buy books simply because they looked good. 1935's *Princess Elizabeth's Gift Book* included colour pages, but on conventional glossy art paper. But the publishers made up for lower production standards with a higher quality of contribution: top writers, and a selection of pieces more specifically aimed at children. Princess Elizabeth was a child and this was *her* Gift Book, compiled for children, sold on behalf of a children's hospital.

In the First World War publishers had been able to produce books of high quality, but no sooner had the Second World War begun than the government imposed severe paper restrictions. All publishers had to eke out their limited stock; large format books with lavish colour illustration were no longer feasible. But if high production standards were out, it was still possible for publishers to commission decent text. Top authors had stepped forward in the First World War – but some had handed in reprints or token contributions: less so with the first, *King Albert's Book*, but increasingly so with the books that followed. For the Second World War such scrappy compilations would not serve.

THE QUEEN'S
BOOK OF THE
RED ✚ CROSS

The first traditional-style Gift Book of the war, *The Queen's Book Of The Red Cross* (1939), switched its emphasis from pictures to text (though it did include top illustrators) and, in a reminder of the skills common to earlier publishers, managed to get into the shops within two months of war's breaking out. It was not the first Gift Book to appear that year: *Rose Window*, published shortly before the war on behalf of **St. Bartholomew's Hospital**, looked like any normal hardback collection of short stories; it *was* illustrated, but only in black & white. Another book, *Soho Centenary* in 1944, dropped the old format altogether, being published on wartime economy paper, in smaller size – but it too did manage to include those all-important illustrations. *Voices On The Green*, produced the following year for a Manchester hospital, was smaller still and, although again confined to black & white illustration, made up for its lack of show by commissioning work from the finest illustrators.

Gift Books continued to be produced after 1945 but, as *Soho Centenary* and *Voices On The Green* demonstrated, the market had declined. Post-war book buyers were less impressed and less likely to respond to a padded-out production (which would have been impossible anyway in the rigorously rationed years after the war) and they no longer saw the purchase of a book as a sensible way to contribute to charity. The minor spending splurges of 1951, Festival of Britain year, and 1953, Coronation year, saw people's money spent on other forms of souvenir: coloured magazines and magazine supplements, along with attendance at associated events, all sold more than books.

In the hedonistic decades that followed, few people thought – and few fund-raisers tried to make them think – there was any good reason they should buy Gift Books. It's true that, in every decade, some books have been bought as *things*, rather than as books to be read, but even when bought as possessions (often to be possessed briefly, while the fad persists) or as things to be given away as gifts, they are not really Gift Books at all. The concept of books as things to be handled, admired and displayed, is a concept that seems to have died with the last century. We still see books sold for charity, but few are lavish: few are presentation volumes. When Oxfam launched its 21st century series of *Ox-Tales*, short stories written for the charity for free by top-name authors, the books were produced in standard paperback format, with no pictures. They were not books to keep. They were to be read, perhaps passed on, then thrown away.

Books, in the 21st century, are more disposable. I wonder whether, in the world of ebooks, there is any future for Gift Books at all. In one sense, perhaps there is. A collection comprising stories, verse or any other written contribution, can just as easily be put together as an ebook and sold for charity as can a traditional book. But it won't be kept. It certainly won't be displayed. It will not, in any real sense, be a Gift Book.

GIFT BOOKS & THEIR CAUSES

A Sequence From 1898 To 1945

'Woman' by W Hatherall – *The Queen's Gift Book*

Gift Books and the causes for which the funds were raised reflect their time. Funds might be raised for charities of a general nature (The National Relief Fund, for example) or for more specific causes – even a particular hospital. The charities most donated to in peacetime are not the same as those in wartime, and throughout the whole of the period of this study, running to 1945, there was no National Health Service and no Welfare State – little help of any kind from the state. Hence the need for charities such as The Printers' Pension Corporation, whose book, *Printers' Pie*, we shall view shortly. That was but one of the many causes which we today would regard as an essential public service but which then relied on charity. But we of the 21st century should not be complacent – not when we rely on charitable donations to fund research into disease and major illnesses, or to provide shelter for the homeless or to feed the hungry.

But to begin at the beginning . . .

The first Gift Book we shall look at was devised to raise funds for a specific London hospital, the second book for Boer War reservists, and the third for private charity. In Edwardian years support was needed for many causes. Then came the war, producing some of our finest Gift Books. Those in the First World War were more lavish than in either the Second or inter-war years, but none of the books are without interest. Most contain fine pictures and all – other than the one mock photograph album – contain submissions by fine and popular writers. And each book is of its time.

Printers'
Pie

1898:WHAT WAS HAPPENING?

This was the year that followed Queen Victoria's Diamond Jubilee, marking the 60th year of her reign. It was the year Emile Zola published his open letter (*J'accuse*) in defence of Dreyfus. China leased Hong Kong to Britain for 99 years, a lease few people thought might ever expire, and in April a Spanish-American War began. Marconi patented radio and in America Mr Kellogg invented cornflakes. Lewis Carroll died.

What was the Good Cause?
The earliest Gift Book in our survey, *Pen and Pencil*, is one of the more unusual. It was put together to raise funds for **The London Hospital.**

Fundraising for this long-established hospital was given a huge shot in the arm when, in 1896, Sydney Holland became its chairman. (He was already chairman of Poplar Hospital.) Year after year he encouraged rich benefactors to make lavish contributions, and his tireless efforts gained him the nickname 'The Prince of Beggars'. The millions of pounds he raised would help transform an East End hospital already much updated to become the largest in the country. Not that it had been insignificant before: founded in 1740; re-sited to Whitechapel in 1757 to become London's finest; extended several times; extended again in 1876 to allow it to take almost 800 patients; given a Medical College and Nursing Home the following year; improved again with a new frontage in 1890; it was the perfect project for this energetic man. (He became Viscount Knutsford in 1914. Getting national newspapers and magazines involved in the Press Bazaar campaign and Gift Book was one of his more modest fund-raising schemes.)

Queen Alexandra was particularly fond of the hospital and did much to support it and, later, in 1913, she lent her name to the establishment of the **Alexandra Rose Day** in aid of *all* hospitals. (It continues to this day.) The East End hospital continued to expand both in size and medical technique throughout the 20th century, becoming part of the NHS in 1948 and being renamed the Royal London in 1990. It has now merged with two others, St Bartholomew's and the London Chest Hospital, under the clumsy aegis of the Barts and The London NHS Trust.

PEN AND PENCIL

A Souvenir of the "Press Bazaar"
Compiled and arranged by the Proprietors of "Punch",
the "Daily Graphic", and the "Daily Chronicle"
FOR THE BENEFIT OF THE LONDON HOSPITAL
June 28-29, 1898
196 unnumbered pages, 30.5cm x 20cm landscape
format, red board cover blocked in gold.

"PEN AND PENCIL"

A Souvenir of the "Press Bazaar"

♥♥♥

Compiled and arranged by the Proprietors of "Punch," the "Daily Graphic," and
the "Daily Chronicle"

FOR THE BENEFIT OF THE LONDON HOSPITAL

♥♥

June 28—29, 1898

One of the rarest books in this collection, and different in
appearance from most Gift Books both in shape and in
its lack of colour plates, this is a fascinating
amalgamation of pieces from famous late-Victorian
names. Its opening picture, reproducing Briton Riviere's
Requiescat (a sad dog gazing up at the dead armoured
knight, its master), would seem more suited to the
following century's war-related Gift Books, but the
entries that follow are a splendidly mixed bunch.

Graphic artists include Tenniel, Luke Fildes, Phil
May (with a cartoon: "Pore little feller, are yer lost?"
"No. Boo-hoo, but my muvver is."), Sir Lawrence and,
separately, Lady Tadema and their daughter Anna Alma,
Linley Sambourne, G F Watts, Lewis Baumer, Leonard
Raven-Hill, Bernard Partridge, Gordon Browne (twice),

Eyre Crowe, Frank Dicksee, Stampa, Charles and H M Brock, Frank Dadd, Val Prinsep, (the elderly) William Small, and Solomon J Solomon with a reproduction of his famous bare-chested Delilah (actually entitled *Samson*).

A Parable

The Cheese-mites asked how the Cheese got there
And warmly debated the matter
The Orthodox said that it came from the air,
And the Heretics held from the platter.
They argued it long and they argued it strong
And no doubt they are arguing now;
But of all the choice spirits who lived in the cheese
Not one of them thought of a cow

A Conan Doyle.
May 23/98

Authors' contributions, though unillustrated, are given in facsimiles of the authors' handwriting and, as with the graphic artists' works, they are signed, and it is this that gives the book much of its fascination.

The elegant Swinburne scratches with a shaky hand, J M Barrie is illegible, Anne Thackeray Ritchie and George Moore both cross out and change a word. The ailing George Meredith writes from the London Hospital for which funds are being raised. Andrew Lang (of the Red, Blue and various colour *Fairy Books*) submits a memorial to Stevenson in a surprisingly awkward hand.

Among other famous names are Anthony Hope (of *Prisoner of Zenda* fame), Kipling ('Lest we forget' in his own handwriting), Zola (in French, of course), Walter Besant, Conan Doyle, Austin Dobson, Israel Zangwill, George Gissing, Edmund Gosse, George Moore and W E Henley – with, as ever in his own handwriting – the poem that begins:

> *What have I done for you*
> *England, my England?*
> *What is there I would not do,*
> *England my own?*

The last word comes from Arthur Balfour, Leader of the Commons, though not yet Prime Minister – a man famed for his avoidance of handwriting (he was myopic) but still prepared to point out, in a perfectly sound hand, that:

> *The richest city in the world should find*
> *no difficulty in providing whatever funds*
> *are required to support a hospital*
> *destined to the service of its poorest*
> *citizens.*

They are words that we in the 21st century would do well to remember.

THE ABSENT-MINDED BEGGAR

By Rudyard Kipling
The Whole Proceeds From The Sale Of This Poem
Will Be Devoted By The "Daily Mail"
In The Name Of Rudyard Kipling,
To The Benefit Of The
Wives And Children Of The Reservists

Copyright in England and the United States by the Daily Mail Publishing Co., 1899

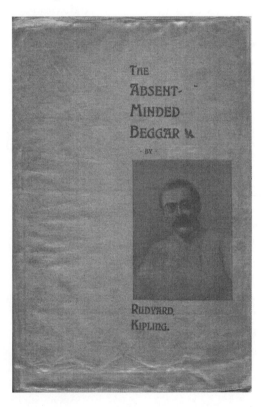

A 3-sheet gate-fold document printed on pale gold satin-like material (versions were also available printed on paper) and measuring 18.5cm x 29cm per sheet (thus 56.5cm x 29cm unfolded). Printed in brown, it carried Kipling's portrait on the front, a drawing by Caton Woodville inside, and an Eyre & Spottiswoode "royal" crest to the outside rear.

Though not a Gift Book as such and therefore not truly eligible for this survey, this attractive item is an early example of a gift item being sold at a premium price with all profits going to charity – in this case to the support of reservists fighting in the Boer War.

The poem is printed on the second and fourth sheet in facsimile handwriting, with Woodville's full-page cartoon intervening. The poem begins:

> *When you've shouted "Rule Britannia"*
> *When you've sung "God Save the Queen"*
> *When you've finished killing Kruger with*
> *your mouth –*
> *Will you kindly drop a shilling in my little*
> *tambourine*
> *For a gentleman in <u>kharki</u> ordered south?*

"A gentleman in kharki."

(As can be seen from the cartoon, 'kharki' was the preferred spelling throughout.)

1903: What Was Happening?

This year saw the first regular transatlantic radio broadcast between the US and England, and the announcement of a new bicycle race: the Tour de France. Having begun the year by proclaiming King Edward VII as Emperor of India, in March colonialist British subdued some rebellious Africans and assumed control of 500,000 square miles of northern Nigeria. At home Emmeline Pankhurst, as part of the fight for women's rights, formed the Women's Social and Political Union. In America, Niagara Falls ran out of water because of a drought, the Wright brothers obtained an airplane patent, and Henry Ford incorporated a company he called Ford Motors. A military coup d'état occurred in Serbia.

What was the Good Cause?
Our cause for 1903 is more narrowly focussed than are most of the charities helped by books covered here, but is a worthy one nevertheless, one which sought support from both its own trade and the general public. The **Printers' Pension Corporation** (established in 1827) launched what was, for a while, to become the annual publication of a fund-raising magazine/book, "Printer's Pie":

It has been suggested that the title is one which needs explanation. Pie, in the ordinary sense, denotes a dish containing various palatable ingredients, but in a printing-office signifies good "matter" thrown together in confusion by a careless or incompetent printer. I feel sure that those who read this volume will class it under the first category with regard to the contributions, but fear that as far as editing goes it will be placed in the second: in fact one eminent editor, when the scheme was mentioned to him, was good enough to describe it as "an incompatible menagerie".

Nevertheless, the said editor, Mr W Hugh Spottiswoode, continued:

It has been the custom lately for every new book or periodical to be launched with a Mission. Frankly the Mission of this volume is to transfer as many half-crowns as possible from the pockets of the public to the funds of the Printers' Pension Corporation.

Half a crown was perhaps too high a sum to ask, as in year two (1904) the price of the annual dropped to a shilling. But their motives were good, Mr Spottiswoode reassured his potential customers, using the words of Lord Glenesk:

The Printers' Pension Corporation was started in 1827 by two compositors who, in setting up the rules of the Watchmakers' Pension Society, thought that their own trade should have a pension fund. They thereupon set to work to found one. It went on and grew from year to year, and some £110,000 has now been distributed in pensions. They have 261 pensioners, a large almshouse, and an asylum for orphans – all happy and thriving. ("setting up" in this case meant setting up text in type.)

Everyone gave their services for free – the authors, the artists, "the Engravers, the Paper Makers, the Ink Manufacturers, the Printers, the Binders, and the Publishers" – and a high-class job they all made of it, for each of the several years the publication continued.

Printers' Pie

A Festival Souvenir of the
Printers' Pension, Almshouse and Orphan Asylum
Corporation, 1903 (and subsequently, 1904, 1905 et cetera).
Published at the offices of "The Sphere"
Great New Street, London

The initial (1903) edition had 72 pages, 22cm x 28cm, with coloured card covers, but the number of pages varied from 72 in 1903 to 112 in 1907.

As one would expect from an eminent printing trade publication the production standards were high (although the 1907 edition was printed on an inferior paper which has browned over time). The initial volume adopted a classy-looking but not very reader-friendly pseudo-archaic style of paragraph breaks in which breaks were signified by the traditional paragraph symbol ¶ – favoured by The Kelmscott Press and others – but this affectation was dropped in later editions (along with the price-drop from 2/6 to 1/-) no doubt to increase the appeal of the publication to general readers. Each issue came with fine illustrations, often full-page and several of which were full-colour plates tipped in.

Artists included well-known illustrators such as Lawson Wood, Raven Hill, Charles Dana, Harry Furniss, Phil May, H M Bateman and John Hassall, along with more conventional names such as John Lavery, Edwin Abbey, Sir Edward Poynter, Lewis Baumer and Cecil Aldin. There were also more traditional plates reproducing the work of George Romney and the like. Authors included Thomas Hardy, Jerome K Jerome, E V Lucas, William le Queux, Ouida, Mrs Braddon, George R Sims, Barry Pain, Katharine Tynan and Israel Zangwill – an author always placed last in the alphabetical list of contents, and to whom the editor several times apologised.

1905: What Was Happening?

A quiet year for Britain. The first RAC Tourist Trophy was run on the Isle of Man and, for those whose sporting tastes were more sedate, the first Australian Tennis Open took place. Campbell-Bannerman became Prime Minister. The Russian Tsar said he would allow the Polish people to speak Polish and, for different reasons, Russia itself suffered increasing internal dissent. The Russia-Japanese War continued, and Russian sailors mutinied on the battleship Potemkin. The glamorous actresses Clara Bow and Greta Garbo were born, and the benefactor Doctor Barnardo died, having had 60,000 children pass through his care.

What was the Good Cause?
In 1905 the country was much exercised by the problem of unemployment. In August the government passed an Unemployed Workmen Bill, to be followed in December by the appointment of a Royal Commission on the Poor Law and the Unemployed. But the need for relief remained. No surprise then that Queen Alexandra was applauded for instituting **The Royal Fund for the Unemployed**. Hers and the London Unemployed Fund were among several such charities in existence. But in the early years of the last century the poor received little assistance from the state (even the Old Age Pension was not introduced until 1908).

THE QUEEN'S CHRISTMAS CAROL

An Anthology of Poems, Stories, Essays, Drawings and Music by British Authors, Artists and Composers
Published by the "Daily Mail": London, Manchester & Paris 1905
In aid of the Royal Fund for the Unemployed
– or, as page iii has it:
'*as a Tribute of Music, Art, and Letters to Her gracious appeal on behalf of the poorest of Her people.*'
128 pages, 22cm x 28cm, cream cloth-bound cover blocked in green

Fred Pegram's sketch for *The Queen's Christmas Carol*

A nice touch to this relatively early gift book comes straight after the title page, where a double-sided page displays signatures from each of the contributors. Authors to the compilation include Alfred Austin (Poet Laureate), Albert Chevalier (with a music hall song, *The Workhouse Man*), Marie Corelli (who supplies a pious piece on *The Spirit of Work*), Arthur Pinero (remembering *A Supper With Irving*), W W Jacobs (describing *Wapping-on-Thames*), Arthur Morrison (with a typical *Christmas in Mean Streets*) and *A Carol of Christmas* 'by A Jew' (Israel Zangwill).

Pictures come from Lawrence Alma-Tadema (a dull and not at all titillating pencil portrait), Sir Edward Poynter (a more interesting pencil sketch), Solomon J Solomon (a fairly hideous baby painting), Edwin Abbey, Linley Sambourne (*A Quiet Piper* looking anything but quiet), Holman Hunt (an 1892 desert sketch), Fred Pegram and Frederic Shields (earthbound angels), and the cartoonists Tom Browne, Bernard Partridge and Louis Wain. Poems appear from Swinburne and Watts-Dunton, W S Gilbert, Austin Dobson, Alice Meynell, Thomas Hardy and Bram Stoker. Musical interludes come from Sir Edward Elgar (supplying the full music for a pianoforte sketch, *In Smyrna*), Edward German (with a similar if shorter score for a *Melody in F*), Sir Alexander Mackenzie (*Ring Out, Wild Bells*) and Sir Herbert Oakeley ('Composer for Scotland to HM King Edward VII' with *A New Year Chorale)*.

'A Quiet Piper' - Linley Sambourne, for *The Queen's Christmas Carol*

1908: What Was Happening?

Prime Minister Campbell-Bannerman resigned because of ill health. Asquith succeeded him. Lloyd George presented his first budget, introducing the old age pension. London hosted the Olympic Games, and the exotic dancer Maud Allan packed theatres. In America, the first Ford Model T automobile was built (and sold for $825). Bulgaria declared independence; Austria annexed Bosnia & Herzegovina; Serbia and Montenegro signed an anti-Austria-Hungarian pact. Albert Einstein presented his quantum theory of light.

What was the Good Cause?
While all the other Gift Books are specific in naming which charity the funds will go to, this early one is an exception, being sold merely 'for charity'. Presumably the Queen's name was quite enough. She was known to be an indefatigable worker for charity.

QUEEN ALEXANDRA'S CHRISTMAS GIFT BOOK

Photographs From My Camera
To be Sold for Charity
Published by "The Daily Telegraph" London 1908
22cm x 29cm, cream cloth-bound cover blocked in green

Whether the Queen actually took these photographs is uncertain but the book was produced to resemble a typical family snapshot album, with 2 or 3 actual photos tipped in to each of 16 dark, cartridge paper pages and with brief captions supplied on tissue paper interleaves. Between these facsimile pages are a further 16 double-sided white pages of conventionally printed photographs, though they inevitably lack the apparent verisimilitude and charm of their companions. Photographs show members of the royal family and their party on board ship or holidaying at Balmoral or on travels around the Empire. Many of the shots have a pleasing informality, though the one allowable exception is the frontispiece, a full-page portrait of the Queen taken by the firm of W&D Downey. Among the apparently spontaneous shots are some of European royalty ('Duke of Sparta in his garden at Athens', 'Charles and little Olav', 'The little Caesarevitch and his Sailor Friend', etc.).

'The Little Caesarevitch' from *Queen Alexandra's Christmas Gift Book*

Acknowledgements are made to the printers and publishers, but also to an astonishing 22 shipping lines, as well as to '*KODAK LIMITED (whose Kodaks were used by Her Majesty), for placing their extensive system of distribution at the Publisher's disposal.*'

1914: What Was Happening?

The First World War began on August 4th 1914, and one of the first actions was Germany's invasion of Belgium. Refugees fled out from Belgium across Europe. Many who came to Britain brought with them tales of horror and despoliation. The British people felt an unprecedented wave of sympathy and alliance with their Belgian neighbours, for Brave Little Belgium had been invaded and despoiled by Giant Germany. To the fierce patriotism of the British, newly at war, was added outrage and sympathy.

What was the Good Cause?
It is hard for some of us today to empathise with that wave of sympathy. It was borne along in part by an undertow of bellicose patriotism but was carried further by a swell of first-hand experience. A quarter of a million Belgian refugees poured in through Britain's ports to escape the advancing German Army: the largest refugee movement in British history. The stories the refugees told were terrible – and by the time they were reported in the Press they became more terrible still. On the eve of war Germany had implemented the Schlieffen plan, sending her troops into Belgium and Luxemburg and violating the 1839 Treaty of London, under which Britain had guaranteed Belgian neutrality.

To dissuade Belgian civilians from resorting to guerrilla warfare, Germany executed suspect Belgian civilians and burnt and pillaged Belgian property. For two months, from the 4th of August until the 9th of October when German troops entered the city, Antwerp found itself besieged by the German Army. During the siege of Antwerp many civilians fled via the ports along the coast, crossing either into the Netherlands, only to be interned, or sailing from Rotterdam to Britain. Belgians in the south of the country fled into France.

Britain willingly received these Belgian refugees, though so many came that they had to be dispersed throughout the country. Responsibility for the relief and housing of Belgian refugees devolved to local government boards and sub-committees. **The Belgian Relief Fund** was but one of the ways in which much needed money was raised to house, clothe and feed the refugees.

One of the fund-raising tools was *King Albert's Book*.

KING ALBERT'S BOOK

A Tribute To The Belgian King And People From Representative Men And Women Throughout The World published by The Daily Telegraph for Christmas 1914 in conjunction with the Daily Sketch, the Glasgow Herald and Hodder and Stoughton 188 pages, 22cm x 28cm, ivory cloth-bound cover blocked in black

Unlucky Albert's glum face stands in opposition to the title page, and it was to unlucky – or as she was then more commonly called – plucky Belgium, the first country invaded by Germany in the First World War, that the book sought to bring *'in this solemn moment when her heart is cruelly and almost incurably wounded, the expression of our Love, our sympathy, and our unbounded admiration, as the spiritual message of the civilised world to the suffering millions of her people, in the midst of the ruin and desolation which still lie heavy upon her even at this sacred Season – when the holiest aspirations of humanity are towards peace on earth and good-will to men.'*

King Albert's Book was the first wartime Gift Book, produced in a style reminiscent of earlier Hodder and Stoughton Gift Books, a style which would be copied for several more books as war went on. It remains the archetypal Gift Book, the one most commonly found today, but none the worse for that as it was produced to a high standard and contains much of interest to us still. Belgium's swift fall and the frequently exaggerated, often untrue, tales of horror and barbarity supposedly inflicted on her people by an again supposedly brutish invader had whipped the British public into what Lord Macaulay, long before, had called 'one of its periodical fits of morality':

"With nothing to gain by taking up arms, with no territory to annex, no commerce to capture, no injury to revenge, having neither part nor lot in any European quarrel, desiring only to be left alone that she might pursue the arts of peace, Belgium found herself suddenly confronted by the choice of allowing her soil to be invaded by a powerful neighbour on his way to destroy his enemy, or of protecting her independence as a separate nation by the whole strength of her armed resistance.

"Although one of the smallest and least aggressive of the countries of Europe, the daughter among the nations, Belgium, true to her lofty political idealism, chose the latter part, not counting the cost, only realising that a ruthless crime was about to be committed, and drawing the sword, after the sword had been drawn against her, in defence of her honour, her national integrity, her right to be mistress in her own house, her historic heritage of freedom and all the spiritual traditions of race. . ."

Hall Caine's Introduction runs on in this vein for two and a half pages, and the opening contribution of the book itself, a handwritten facsimile from Prime Minister Asquith, maintains the mood, beginning, *'The Belgians have won for themselves the immortal glory which belongs to a people who prefer freedom to ease, to security, even to life itself.'*

Turn the page and you find four more paeans to the Belgians, from the Archbishop of Canterbury, the Aga Khan, Edmond Rostand (a leading French dramatist) and Arthur Balfour. Turn to the next page and you meet the French, Russian and Japanese ambassadors. In such exalted company who could refuse to contribute to the book? After two pages from the Earl of Rosebery we find our first poem, from Rudyard Kipling ('The Outlaws', made copyright in November 1914: as we will find, many of the contributions were written specifically for this book). The Queen's portrait lies on a page opposite three more notes from statesmen, and John Lavery's painting is in turn followed by a poem from Thomas Hardy.

Among many notables encountered in the following pages are Winston Churchill (with an uncharacteristically short piece in which he predicts that Belgium's future will be 'more brilliant than any which she could ever have planned'), David Lloyd George

(Chancellor of the Exchequer, not yet Prime Minister), Earl Kitchener, Arnold Bennett, Bonar Law, Sir Arthur Pinero (playwright), John Galsworthy, Andrew Carnegie, the philosopher Henri Bergson, the Chief Rabbi and the Cardinal Archbishop of Reims. The prolific Mrs Humphrey Ward presents a piece on 'All Saints' Day 1914', an unexpected if uncontroversial contribution comes from leading suffragette Emmeline Pankhurst, and in 'Some Eugenic Ideals' Sir James Barr expresses views which are, as the title suggests, of their time.

"Plorans ploravit in nocte: et lacrymæ ejus in maxillis ejus ..... Manum suam misit hostis ad omnia desiderabilia ejus." [Lamentatio Jeremiæ Prophetæ 1. 2. 10.]

By BERNARD PARTRIDGE

LA BELGIQUE: 1914.

Famous names continue: Gilbert Murray, Robert Hichens, Edward Carpenter, the 'sensation' novelist Mrs Braddon (in her seventies, she would die the following year), tile-maker and novelist William de Morgan, the legendary Sarah Bernhardt and Camille Saint-Saens. Theirs are two of several entries in French, translated, along with pieces from Anatole France, Maurice Maeterlinck, et cetera. Then comes Baden-Powell, Marconi, Paderewski, Admiral Jellicoe, Augustine Birrell, Jack London, Baroness Orczy (who manages a complete short story in only a page and a half), G K Chesterton (with a rather marvellous reflection on 'The Largest Window in the World'), William Canton, Israel Zangwill and the Irish statesman T P O'Connor. Edmund Gosse writes on 'The Belgian Poets' and Alfred Noyes, like Kipling earlier, provides a specially-written poem, 'The Redemption of Europe'. More verse appears from Ella Wheeler Wilcox, Alice Meynell, Sidney Low, Maurice Hewlett, Eden Phillpotts, the novelist Marie Corelli (who crams ten exclamation marks into her two wince-making verses), W L Courtney, the Italian Annie Vivanti Chartres, Owen Seaman, May Sinclair (better known for her 'stream of consciousness' novels), Edith Wharton (American novelist, not known for her poetry) and Walter Sichel. Sir Herbert Beerbohm Tree writes a 4-page patriotic playlet.

'A Study' by Harrison Fisher

Tipped-in coloured plates are provided by Sir
Edward Poynter, Frank Dicksee, Sir Luke Fildes, Sir
William Blake Richmond, Sir E A Waterlow, Briton
Riviere, Arthur Rackham, W L Bruckman (a Dutch
artist), Edmund Dulac, Kay Nielsen, John Collier ('*A
Glass of Wine with Caesar Borgia*' – the title tells it all),
J J Shannon, Harrison Fisher (whose painting of an
attractive girl is typical of the Harrison portraits on many
postcards of the time), and A D McCormick. Black and
white illustrations come from Solomon J Solomon,
Chandler Christy (a young and contemporary angel

waving her hands over a remarkably clean-shaven fallen soldier 'On the Field of Honour'), Sir Thomas Brock (a far more sombre sketch than one might expect: '*I offer my picture as a small tribute to the splendid courage and fortitude shown by the Belgian people in upholding the honour and integrity of their country, offering as they do an example to the whole world*'), Walter Crane (who supplies a poem also), Seymour Lucas, J Montgomery Flagg, Joseph Pennell, William Nicholson, cartoonist Leonard Raven-Hill and fellow cartoonist Bernard Partridge with his serious 'La Belgique: 1914'.

American artists also appear: Charles Dana Gibson (though he doesn't give us one of his 'Gibson Girls') and Maxfield Parrish (with a 'Dies Iræ'). Claude Monet provides words only, but not a picture. Musical settings come from Alexander C Mackenzie (a Browning poem), André Messager (Victor Hugo's 'Pour La Patrie'), F H Cowen (setting Galsworthy's poem, 'A Hymn to Belgium'), Ethel Smythe (fiery British composer, with her own 'March of the Women'), Edward Elgar (a special 8-page 'Chantons, Belges, Chantons!'), Liza Lehmann, Charles Stanford, Edward German (a brief 'Homage to Belgium, 1914'), Debussy ('Berceuse Héroïque'), the Norwegian Backer-Lunde, the Danish Lange-Müller, and the Italian Pietro Mascagni.

It is a war-strewn, emotional and patriotic book, outraged and indignant on behalf of 'little Belgium' but, having so many notable contributors, it cannot fail to intrigue anyone who flicks through its clearly printed pages. Some pieces, inevitably, now seem dull, with little of interest other than their facsimile signatures, but others can be both entertaining and illuminating. You will surely recognize the names of many of these famed contributors but, without this book, you may not have actually read any of their words. Here you can.

By L. RAVEN-HILL
"You mark my word Jarge ; that there Kayser 'll come to
a bad end : I've 'ad my eye on un for many a day !"

Leonard Raven-Hill's

"You mark my word, Jarge; that there Kayser'll come to a bad
end. I've 'ad my eye on un for many a day!"

Another Wartime Cause:

The Queen's 'Work For Women' Fund

The Queen was Mary (1867-1953), wife of King George V, whom she had married in 1893. She was mother to the 17-year-old Princess Mary (full title HRH The Princess Victoria Alexandra Alice Mary) and grandmother to Queen Elizabeth II. Already active in charitable work, Queen Mary had become more so with the outbreak of the First World War, involving herself with the National Relief Fund, Queen Mary's Needlework Guild, the St John Ambulance Brigade and the Red Cross. **The Queen's Work for Women Fund**, which had been established by Queen Alexandra, was the women's branch of the National Relief Fund.

The best known charitable contribution from Princess Mary herself was her Christmas Gift Fund launched on 14 October 1914, which helped create one of the most charming mementos of the First World War – the **Princess Mary's Gift Box**. The young princess had offered to pay for a personal gift to every soldier and sailor out of her private allowance. Clearly impracticable, it was agreed instead that she would lend her name to a public fund to raise the money to provide the gift. Recipients would receive an embossed brass box, one ounce of pipe tobacco, twenty cigarettes, a pipe, a tinder lighter, Christmas card and photograph; non-smokers received the brass box, a packet of acid tablets (sweeties, not LSD!), a khaki writing case containing pencil, paper and envelopes, together with the Christmas card and photograph of the Princess. The Fund was a great success, raising more money than was needed to fulfil the original intention, and would have required more tinder boxes (over half a million) than manufacturers Asprey's could provide. Substitute gifts were hastily created to include bullet pencil cases, tobacco pouches, shaving brushes, combs, pencil cases with packets of postcards, knives, scissors, cigarette cases and purses. Sailors didn't receive a lighter but were given instead a handsome bullet pencil in a silver cartridge case which bore Princess Mary's monogram.

All profits on sale are given to
THE QUEEN'S "WORK FOR WOMEN" FUND
which is acting in conjunction with THE NATIONAL
RELIEF FUND

Published in 1914 by Hodder & Stoughton
140 pages, 18.5cm x 25cm, cream cloth-bound cover
blocked in green

Printed for
Princess Mary's Gift Book
by J. J. Shannon, R.A.

Mary

Facing a frontispiece portrait of the Princess by J J
Shannon is her facsimile signed note on Buckingham
Palace notepaper: '*I desire to express my very best
thanks to those Authors and Artists who have so
generously contributed to my Gift Book.*' (Good to see
Authors and Artists granted capital letters.)
Contributions follow from J M Barrie (whose wry tale,
'A Holiday in Bed' is a long way from *Peter Pan*); G A
Birmingham (comic writer more famous for his Dr
O'Grady character); Hall Caine (dramatist and popular
author – and editor of *King Albert's Book*); Ralph

Connor (whose pious poem is even less to modern taste than is his novel, *The Sky Pilot*); Conan Doyle (keeping well away from Sherlock Holmes by submitting 'Bimbashi Joyce'); J H Fabre (giving us a natural history piece on 'The Ant-Lion', strikingly illustrated by E J Detmold); Ellen Thorneycroft Fowler (with a patriotic 'true story' entitled 'An Angel of God'); Charles Garvice (popular author of the day, with another patriotic story); Lady Sybil Grant (whose children's poem 'The Land of Let'spretend' [sic] is illustrated by Arthur Rackham); Rider Haggard (with a stirring 'Magepa the Buck' illustrated by Byam Shaw); one-time feminist writer Beatrice Harraden invoking Spartan virtues in a tale – illustrated by Dulac – that ends:

'What do you think about this grand old Spartan code of honour? Do you not think that we ourselves, each in our own way, young and old, man and woman, boy and girl, may find something helpful in it to bring to the service of our country?'.

a tailpiece by Claude A Shepperson

Then comes Rudyard Kipling (whose poem 'Big Steamers' sails along with a typically rolling rhythm); the Bishop of London (penning a surprisingly pro-military couple of pages); A E W Mason (with a military romance set in the 1870s); Alfred Noyes (whose poem 'A Spell for a Fairy' is prettily illustrated by Claude A Shepperson); Baroness Orczy (giving us an episode from the adventurous life of her Scarlet Pimpernel); John Oxenham (with a cringe-making poem 'What Can A Little Chap Do?' suggesting that the lad 'can march in the queue of the Good and the Great' or, at the very least, 'can shun all that's mean, He can keep himself clean'); W Pett Ridge (who follows that with a children's story which, as it title suggests, is 'Altogether Different' – and whose leading character, a little girl with spirit, is well caught by Lewis Baumer); Annie S Swan (well-known children's writer, with a suitable 'girl's story from gallant Belgium'); Kate Douglas Wiggin, author of *Rebecca of Sunnybrook Farm* (in whose 'Fleur-de-lis' the impoverished orphan heroine inspires a more fortunate girl to chide her mother with the words, '*I am not as sentimental as you and papa seem to fancy. I am not certain that I ought to wrap that cold little child in my new seal jacket, and run bare-headed by the side of the organ collecting pennies for the poor one-armed man. I know that if I should go down into the slums I should find a thousand others, and if I worked from year's end to year's end, and spent papa's entire fortune, I could not make them all comfortable.*').

Other illustrations are supplied by Russell Flint, C E Brock, H R Millar, Arch Webb, A J Gough, Talbot Kelly, Steven Spurrier, J H Hartley, Norman Wilkinson, Joseph Simpson, W B Wollen, A C Michael, H M Brock, Eugene Hastain, Gordon Browne, M E Gray, Harold Earnshaw, Carlton Smith and Edmund J Sullivan

– a true gallery of early 20th century illustrators.

     This is a nice book to own, though it has to be said that in the century that has passed since it was published, the pages in any edition you may find will almost certainly have foxed a little and turned brown at the edges. But how will *any* of us look, after our own hundredth birthday?

POEMS OF THE GREAT WAR

Published on Behalf of the Prince of Wales' National Relief Fund
published by Chatto and Windus in 1914. 40 pages, paperback Octavo.

This small – and, if you ever find one, fragile – book was printed in association with the *Times* which had printed each of the poems in its newspaper pages shortly before. Poets included Robert Bridges (the Poet Laureate), Henry Newbolt, Maurice Hewlett, Owen Seaman, Laurence Binyon, Rudyard Kipling, Alfred Noyes and G K Chesterton. William Nicholson designed the cover, showing a mother sheltering her baby while her young son, perhaps five years old, struggles to unsheathe his father's sword. The book sold for a shilling.

The book closed with an appeal:

Those who cannot fight for their country can help in quieter ways. One way is to collect money for the Prince of Wales' National Relief Fund. Every purchaser of this book is, in a real sense, a subscriber to the Fund, but his duty does not end there. Let him make it his business to see that at least twelve of his friends buy the book too. That would be really doing something!

1915: What Was Happening?

Few now had illusions about the war. The British Expedition Army in Belgium captured Neuve Chapelle, but Winston Churchill instigated a disastrous assault on the Dardanelles. At the deadly second Battle of Ypres, Germany became the first party to use poison gas. In the Atlantic, a German submarine sank the American *Lusitania* and almost 1,200 people died. In the Autumn Offensive on the Western Front, Britain lost 50,000 men, France 190,000, and Germany 140,000. Asquith's government formed a Coalition with the Tories. The Ford Motor Company made its millionth Model T. Einstein published his General Theory of Relativity.

What was the Good Cause?
St. Dunstan's was established in 1915 by Arthur Pearson, owner of the *Evening Standard* and *Daily Express*, soon after he had become the President of the National Institution for the Blind. He had lost his own sight due to glaucoma. Another early benefactor for the charity was the American Banker, Otto Kahn, who lent his Bayswater Road residence, St Dunstan's Lodge, to Pearson for the duration of the war. In March 1915, sixteen blinded soldiers and sailors were moved in to begin a revolutionary rehabilitation and training programme, designed to help them and those who would follow to lead as normal a life as possible and to earn their own living, rather than be forced to rely on charity.

Originally, when based in Bayswater Road, St. Dunstan's was called the Blind Soldiers and Sailors Hostel, and its name was shortened to St Dunstan's when, in 1921, it moved into St. John's Lodge (later renamed St. Dunstan's Villa) in Regent's Park. By the end of the war over six hundred men had been trained, seven hundred were still in training and two hundred

63

were in the hostel. Further convalescent homes were established at Blackheath, Ilkley, Hastings and Brighton's Kemp Town. When in 1921 Pearson died of an accident at the early age of 55 his place was taken by the 24-year-old Ian Fraser, a 'St. Dunstaner' himself, who had been trained at Regent's Park after having been blinded by a bullet on the Somme in 1916. In 1924 he became Member of Parliament for North St Pancras. He was knighted in 1934 and remained Chairman until his death in 1974.

The work of St. Dunstan's continued in the Second World War, first at new premises in Ovingdean, near Brighton – though these premises had to be abandoned in 1940 due to fears of an imminent invasion – and then in Church Stretton in Shropshire. St Dunstan's returned to Ovingdean after the war in 1946, and now has additional properties in Sheffield and Llandudno, where its work continues to this day.

THE BLINDED SOLDIERS AND SAILORS GIFT BOOK

Published in 1915 by Jarrold & Sons
231 pages, 19cm x 24.5cm, with a decorated, dark sand coloured cloth-bound cover

Jarrold's trip into the Gift Book market follows a similar pattern set by other publishers – famous author contributions interspersed with line, offset and tipped-in illustrations – although, compared to some, this compilation contains a great deal of material concerned specifically with the war. George Goodchild's Foreword assures the purchaser:

All profits accruing from the sale of the present volume will be set aside and handed over to Mr. C. Arthur Pearson for the benefit of the brave fellows at St. Dunstan's; and every purchaser of this volume may feel that he or she has directly contributed towards the welfare of those who have sacrificed so much in defence of our national ideals.

Robert Hichens kicks off the volume with 'In The Dark', beginning:

'Until I became a special constable and took to patrolling by night, I did not realise that there are a great many people who never allow themselves to be in the dark, a great many people who cannot even sleep without a light in the room.'

G K Chesterton pens a typically offbeat piece on 'Shakespeare and the Germans' ('. . . *just as France has, on the whole, encouraged whatever is liberal and intellectual, it is not too much to say that Germany has encouraged what is illiberal and especially what is literal. The German professors have done a great many devastating things; but perhaps the worst thing about them was that they were the first to understand Shakespeare. It is a great impertinence to understand Shakespeare: for Shakespeare certainly did not understand himself. . .* ' et cetera).

Arnold White, T P O'Connor, Sir Laurence Gomme and A C Benson provide thought pieces of their own, and Charles Marriott writes on St Dunstan's itself, with photographs of the new Blinded Soldiers' and Sailors' Hostel. Short stories come from Walter Emanuel, John Galsworthy, Ellen Thorneycroft Fowles, J E Patterson, H G Wells (reprinting his earlier 'The Land Ironclads' which predicted the use of tanks in warfare), Beatrice Harraden, Keble Howard and A Burfield.

As well as two concluding sonnets from John Milton (including, inevitably, 'When I consider how my light is spent') there are poems from Edmund Gosse, Austin Dobson, Gilbert Parker, E Nesbit, W L Courtney, Guy Thorne, Evelyn Underhill and A St John Adcock. Barry Pain presents 'Two Little Fables' and Anthony Hope throws in a review sketch ('Smoke Rings', which has nothing to do with the war). Full plates come from Hugh Thomson, Harry Folkard, Charles Folkard, Claude A Shepperson, C E Brock, W H Caffyn, Cyrus Cuneo, R L Knowles, W Heath Robinson, Sir Luke Fildes, Lewis Baumer, F H Townsend, Frank Brangwyn and Frank Wright.

'A Relic of the Fight' by Frank Wright

Among all the tragical figures of the war none are more deserving of our sympathy and help than those whose injuries – received in defence of the Empire – are of the nature of permanent blindness . . .
(from George Goodchild's Foreword to the book)

1915 . . . Campaigns continued on the Home Fronts:

MELBA'S GIFT BOOK

of Australian Art and Literature
Published on behalf of the Belgian Relief Fund by
Hodder and Stoughton / George Robertson & Co
(Australia) in 1915
(actually printed in Great Britain by Hazell, Watson &
Viney Ltd.)
124 pages plus 4 prelims, 18cm x 24.5cm, green cloth-
bound cover blocked in green

You cheer for the Belgian heroes,
You gibe at the German gun,
You rave about Modern Neros,
But tell me—what have you done ?
They turned from the Kaiser wooing
With promise of peace and pelf;
You shout with joy for their doing—
But what have you done yourself?

(from 'Help Her Now!' by D W McCay)

Rather harder to find than many Gift Books (or certainly so in Great Britain), it contains an attractive frontispiece portrait of Melba by Florence Rodway, a 'Word of Explanation' by Melba herself and approaching 40 entries contributed by Australian writers, all of which conclude with a relevant facsimile signature. More striking are the many illustrations from artists including Norman Lindsay, Ida Rentoul Outhwaite and David Low.

There are strong tipped-in colour plates from George Lambert, Hans Heysen, George Dancey, Arthur Streeton, E Phillips Fox, Fred C McCubbin and Julian Ashton, and monochrome plates from Hal Gye, Charles Nuttall, Alex Colquhoun, Ellis Rowan, Tom Shield and Esther Paterson. Along with etchings from Victor Cobb, Sydney Ure Smith, Alfred Coffey, Lionel Lindsay, John Shirlow and Percy Leason are some particularly fine black and white tailpieces by different artists. The sculptors Bertram Mackennal, C Douglas Richardson and Margaret Baskerville are represented by photographed statues ('Circe', 'The Tired Dancer' and a winsome 'The Dawn of the Mind').

'The First Lesson' by Ida Rentoul Outhwaite

They rise, a shining legion,
To scale for glory-heights –
Australia in their vanguard
With deathless valour flights.
(the conclusion to
'In The Vanguard'
by Roderic Quinn)

Queen Mary's Convalescent Auxiliary Hospitals

Funds raised for this charity helped create the Queen Mary's Convalescent Auxiliary Hospital, Roehampton, in May 1915: a hospital for sailors, soldiers and airmen who had lost limbs in war service. Far from a mere convalescent hospital, Roehampton rapidly pioneered ground-breaking techniques in amputation, prosthetics, infection control and rehabilitation. A second hospital was set up in Sidcup in 1917. So bloody was the First World War that it is estimated that some 240,000 British servicemen lost a limb.

THE QUEEN'S GIFT BOOK

*in aid of Queen Mary's Convalescent Auxiliary
Hospitals*
*for soldiers and sailors who have lost their limbs in the
war.*

Published in 1915 by Hodder and Stoughton
160 pages, 18cm x 24.5cm, blue cloth-bound cover
blocked in dark blue

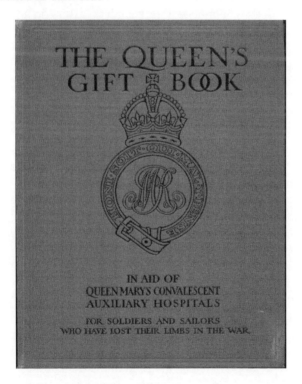

The format is similar to the same publisher's other Gift
Books. A painted portrait of the Queen supplies the
frontispiece, a famous author (Galsworthy) supplies the

foreword, and a galaxy of contemporary writers and artists provide the text – beginning with Arthur Balfour on 'The Pleasures of Reading' (a piece originally penned almost 30 years before).

J M Barrie's light tale, 'The New Dramatist', comes with drawings by Baumer, and E F Benson's story, 'Jill's Cat', has drawings from Harry Rountree. Conrad describes 'The Heroic Age' (by which he meant October 1805 and Nelson), John Buchan's 'Divus Johnston' is a curious tale of Empire, while the tale that follows by J E Buckrose is a domestic comedy that ends with 'the distant, unmistakable sound of a kiss in the attic.' Ethel M Dell does her bit for the war effort with 'The Magic Circle', illustrated by Russell Flint and E H Shepard, and Conan Doyle supplies a poem ('Ypres') accompanied by drawings from Raven-Hill. Jefferey Farnol's 'Journey's End', Joseph Hocking's 'The Failure', and Gilbert Parker's 'Norah' are domestic tales, Leonard Merrick's 'The Fairy Poodle' is a touch more whimsical, and the once fiery Beatrice Harraden supplies 'The Soot-Fairies' alongside a colour plate and two large black-and-whites from Arthur Rackham.

Jerome K Jerome provides a sentimental 'Portrait of a Lady', while John Oxenham's 'Victory Day' begins '*As sure as God's in his Heaven, As sure as He stands for Right, As sure as the hun this wrong hath done, So surely we win this fight!*' (The hun, note, does not get a capital letter.) More conventional stories come from Neil Munro ('Old Brand') and 'Somerville & Ross' ('The Dane's Breechin') while two poets get top illustrators: Lady Clifford is given W Heath Robinson, and Marjory Royce wins brother Charles Robinson and M E Gray. 'Sapper' writes 'a tale from the trenches' and Maud Diver's poem 'He Comes' looks back to the Indian wars. Ernest Thompson Seton's 'The Cubhood of Wahb' is an ill-fitting snippet about grizzly bears and a bull, while Mrs Humphry Ward's 'The Little Goatherd' is a curious classical fantasy warmed by Italian sunshine and a full-page plate from Dudley Hardy – a long, long way from the war.

Other full-page painted portraits in the book present His Majesty The King, His Royal Highness The Prince of Wales, and this hagiographic study of a nurse on the battlefield entitled simply 'Woman'. (By W Hatherell, it accompanies a poem from Hall Caine.) C M Padday portrays 'The Heroic Age'. Other drawings come from Arch Webb, J H Hartley, S Abbey, G Barrow, Leopold Bates, Fred Pegram, Edmund Blampied, Gordon Browne, Claude A Shepperson and C E Brock.

The International Cause:

The Red Cross

What we think of as the Red Cross is, in fact, a group of associated organisations born out of the original ICRC (International Committee of the Red Cross), which was itself a private humanitarian institution founded in Geneva in 1863 and still flourishing. To help overcome any obstacles caused by the apparently Christian ethos of the original charity an International Committee of Red Cross *and Red Crescent* Societies (IFRC) was formed as early as 1919, and from that beginning there are now approaching 200 National Red Cross and Red Crescent Societies actively continuing the work.

The First World War presented the ICRC with enormous challenges as it struggled to provide medical support services and aid to all countries involved in what was then an unprecedented European conflict. One of their first actions was to set up an International Prisoners-of-War Agency and, as part of their work, to inspect prisoner-of-war camps throughout the war. At the same time the ICRC monitored compliance with the terms of the Geneva Convention and with the less well-known Hague Convention of 1907.

The objectives of the ICRC today remain much as they were in the First World War, namely:

- to monitor compliance of warring parties with the Geneva Conventions
- to organize nursing and care for those who are wounded on the battlefield
- to supervise the treatment of prisoners of war
- to help with the search for missing persons in an armed conflict (a tracing service)
- to organize protection and care for civil populations
- to arbitrate between warring parties in an armed conflict

Their activities included rest stations, hospitals, staff and technical assistance, VADs and ambulances – indeed, it was the ICRC that provided the motorised ambulances which eventually replaced the slow horse-drawn ones sent out at the beginning of the First World War. They set up letter and postcard services throughout the war zones and camps and, as the conflict drew to a close, the charity's work actually increased: it now had to help deal with the worldwide outbreak of Spanish Flu, a scourge that would, in turn, kill another two million people. In the immediate post-war years the ICRC ran an efficient tracing service to reunite families separated by war.

The French Red Cross

The French Red Cross was one of the five national societies that, on 5 May 1919 in Paris, founded what was at the time called the League of Red Cross Societies. During the war itself the French Red Cross had operated hospitals both close to the front and behind the lines, and had worked in surprisingly close cooperation with Britain – partly and perversely because British bureaucratic prejudice and obstructiveness had pushed many British women to work directly under the banner of the French Red Cross. Within weeks of war breaking out, when the dunderheaded War Office refused their offer of female help, Dr. Louisa Garrett Anderson and Dr. Flora Murray established a Women's Hospital Corps facility to treat wounded British and French soldiers. So close did the cooperation between the British and French Red Cross become that there seems not to have been a single French Red Cross hospital without British women working in it.

EDMUND DULAC'S PICTURE BOOK FOR THE FRENCH RED CROSS

All Profits On Sale Given To The Croix Rouge Francaise, Comité de Londres
Published for the *Daily Telegraph* by Hodder and Stoughton
136 pages, 21.5cm x 28cm, dark cream cloth-bound cover blocked in dark blue/black

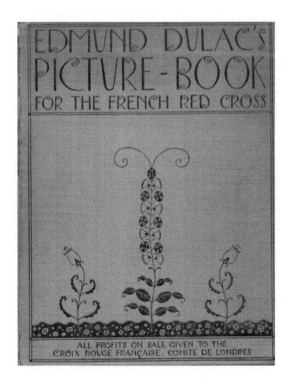

As beautiful a book as one would expect from Dulac's hand, its 17 written pieces are accompanied by 21 tipped-in coloured plates by Dulac and a photograph of the artist himself. Though the appeal is specifically for the *French* Red Cross, British readers are reassured by its having a British address (9 Knightsbridge, London SW), royal patronage (HM Queen Alexandra) and an exhortation to send 'anything you can afford' to the very British *Daily Telegraph*, London EC. The need is clear:

You must remember that everything to do with sick and wounded has to be kept up to a daily standard. It is you who give who provide the drugs, medicines, bandages, ambulances, coal, comfort for those who fight, get wounded, or die to keep you safe. Remember that besides fighting for France, they are fighting for the civilised world, and that you owe your security and civilisation to them as much as to your own men and the men of other Allied Countries.

There is not one penny that goes out of your pockets in this cause that does not bind France and Britain closer together. From the millionaire we need his thousands; from the poor man his store of pence. We do not beg, we insist, that these brave wounded men shall lack for nothing. We do not ask of you, we demand of you, the help that must be given.

There is nothing too small and nothing too large but we need it.

The frontispiece to Edmund Dulac's *Picture Book For the French Red Cross*: Asenath

Some of the stories would be familiar to British readers; some would not. One comes from China, one from Persia, one from Egypt; one tells of Cerberus, one is the 'old world idyll' of Aucassin and Nicolette, and there are three stories from the *Thousand and One Nights*. There is a carol (*Three Kings of Orient*) and four French songs (*Young Rousselle, The Little Seamstress, My Lisette* and *The Chilly Lover*). Accompanying these are 2 Hans Andersen fairy stories, *The Nightingale* and *The Real Princess*, together with *Cinderella* and *Blue Beard*:

Her first impulse was to flee from the spot;—then there came a dreadful thought, and she stayed. Whose bodies were those hanging in the forbidden cupboard? She took a step forward and inspected them more closely. Yes, they were women, and they had been young and beautiful. O horror of horrors! Could it be true? Were those the bodies of Blue Beard's wives, who had disappeared, one after another, so mysteriously? There they hung, spiked through the neck, their feet dangling above pools of their life's blood,—mute evidence of foul murder.

(Just the thing to send the little ones off to sleep.)

A Dulac illustration to 'Bluebeard'

1918: PEACE AT LAST

At the end of the war Britain had suffered some two and a half million casualties, if one includes the 170,000 still held as prisoners of war. 723,000 had been killed and a far greater residue, in excess of 1.6 million, were wounded. Limbs had been lost, men were blinded, countless thousands had their lives shortened from the effects of poison gas. French casualties were higher, Russian higher still, and German casualties outreached both. Casualties from the defeated Austria-Hungary were highest of all (almost 7 million).

Fast on the heels of war came the pitiless scourge of influenza; the great flu epidemic is estimated to have taken the lives of even more people than were killed by the war itself. Yet the charitable appeals and press coverage concentrated on only those killed or maimed in the fighting, as if to have died of flu were somehow shameful: a non-combatant's death, no death for heroes. The Royal Family assumed what has become their traditional role, to make themselves both visible and touchable, a consolatory, even cheering presence. In August 1919 the young Prince of Wales, at that time perhaps the most popular member of the family, set out on a Royal Tour of Canada and America, followed in 1920 by an Australasian Tour.

A decade and a half earlier Queen Alexandra had published a successful photographic record of her less arduous travels to Balmoral. Could not the Prince repeat her success with a book of his own, commemorating his travels about the Empire?

THE PRINCE OF WALES' BOOK

Published for St. Dunstan's
by Hodder & Stoughton
Main pages unnumbered, all 18.2cm x 25cm
Red board covers, embossed with the Prince of Wales
Feathers

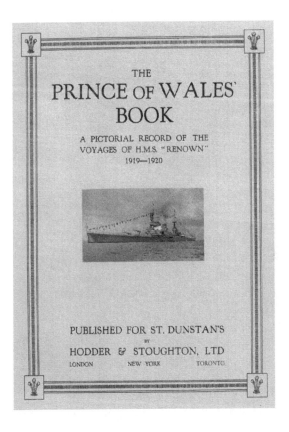

Crammed with rather murky photographs of the two Tours which eclipse the 21 pages of text, the book is an uneasy cross between a pseudo album and photographic record. We see the Prince in naval uniform, dressed as an Indian Chief, in civilian clothes, on horseback, in various cars and on a racecourse. We see him at natural beauty spots, with children and with dignitaries and, above all, among the Empire's armed forces at sea and on land.

At the front of the book is a rather convincing facsimile note in the Prince's handwriting, scrawled across a sheet of writing paper (tipped in and of a smaller size than the pages) headed in red beneath a crest: St James's Palace. S.W. *"I hope that all who can will buy this book of photographs and will thus help me to secure the largest possible assistance for our sailors and soldiers who were blinded in the War."* This is followed by his two-page Introduction, stressing the work done by St Dunstan's hostel for blinded sailors and soldiers, situated as it then was in Regent's Park.

> *"Twelve hundred men have passed through St Dunstan's during the last twelve years. Five hundred are there now or are about to go there very soon. These include 88 Canadians, 81 Australians, 23 New Zealanders, and 13 South Africans. St. Dunstan's has therefore served the Dominions no less than the Old Country, and it has received the most splendid tributes from all those whom it has trained.*
>
> *"I want to call special attention to the word 'trained.' St. Dunstan's is not a hospital, it is a university where men are taught to live again and to enjoy their life despite the loss of sight. Not only does it*

set them up in trades with wonderful success, but it watches and assists them afterwards with materials, with information, and with skilled advice. In this way its utility will continue long after the last of its students has gone out with new hope into the world; and their welfare will depend in large measure upon its ability to keep personal touch with them and to supply their special needs."

1923: What Was Happening?

Europe was nominally at peace, but the effects of the Great War rumbled on. In January, Poland and Lithuania were in conflict, and Poland annexed the Republic of Central Lithuania. In June, Bulgaria's Prime Minister was ousted in a military coup, while elsewhere, China's President Li Yuanhong was ousted by a warlord; in Japan that December, their Crown Prince narrowly survived an assassination attempt in Tokyo.

While most Europeans looked the other way hyperinflation roared through defeated Germany, causing massive unrest and political instability. In November, Adolf Hitler was arrested for his leading role in the Beer Hall Putsch. In 1923 the Treaty of Lausanne brought the Ottoman Empire to an end, the British Mandate for Palestine came into effect, and the Irish Civil War came (notionally) to an end.

In Italy that year, Mount Etna's eruption left 60,000 homeless and when a dam burst on the River Po, 600 people drowned. Meanwhile in America Roy and Walt Disney founded the Walt Disney Company and the famous Hollywood sign appeared on a California hillside. *Time* magazine was launched, and Louis Armstrong cut his first record (*Chimes Blues* with King Oliver's Creole Jazz Band).

What was the Good Cause?

Not all Gift Books were for national or international causes. In August 1923 a small but important hospital far from the centre of British life held a bazaar to raise much-needed funds. **The Balfour Hospital** in Kirkwall in the Orkneys had played its own part in the Great War – as noted by a number of high-ranking Navy men including Admiral Sir F E E Brock: "*I well know the careful service that the Hospital gave to the Fleet during the War, and especially to the Patrol and other vessels based at Kirkwall.*" Another Admiral, Sir Montague Browning, thanked the Hospital and remembered that "*the seamen and Marines borne for duties with the shore batteries and for the local defence were kindly received in the Hospital, and that therefore the Navy owes it a real debt of gratitude.*"

Few in Britain a century later would disagree with the editor of the *Spectator* that year when he wrote "*I most ardently desire that throughout the United Kingdom there should be as large a number as possible of small Hospitals. The Hospital near a poor man's door is worth ten times more to him than a Hospital fifty miles off.*" Today's Minister of Health would do well to mark those words.

THE BOOK OF THE BALFOUR HOSPITAL BAZAAR

published in 1923 by the hospital and printed locally by W R Mackintosh at The Orcadian Office. (*The Orcadian* was the local newspaper.)
120 stapled pages including just 4 pages of advertisements, all pages 18.5cm x 24cm, between green & red paper wrap-round covers, glued to the main text block.

The artist to the striking cover is not credited, and the internal text is different in approach and intention to most Gift Books, being strongly Orkneys themed. ('Rognvald', the man shown on the cover, was a 12th century Norwegian saint and an Earl of Orkney.) Most of the contributions to this book are factual, covering such topics as local birdlife, local history, disappearing flora and fauna, and recollections from local scholars and residents. Poems and occasional pieces of fiction are scattered throughout; typically we find Orkney's Archdeacon writing on *Medicine in Orkney in the 17th Century*, and then a poem, *Oor Auld Milk Horse* (Young Willie who used to drive him having been killed in the War), which is followed in turn by the then celebrated Ian Hay's wartime short story, *The Man Who Had Something Against Him*. After that comes another poem, then *A Viking Ship-Burial* and so the book continues. G K Chesterton is perhaps the most famous contributor but the relative lack of famous names is made up for by the interest of the pieces. Readers who know little of Orkney and its history will find this a fascinating collection.

Bird-lovers will be interested in Alfred Wood's ecologically sad *Notes On Some Rarer Orkney Birds* (including the Sea Eagle and the Great Auk, the Long-Eared and Short-Eared Owls, the Fulmar Petrel and the Red-Necked Phalarope). Walkers and archaeologists may prefer J W Cursiter's account of *The Antiquities of Orkney* while armchair travellers can enjoy Charles MacGreggor's *Memories of Scapa Flow*. Clearly, these are local people (often expert local people) writing on local matters. The book may contain no pictures, but it gives unique views of the Orkneys and its inhabitants of every kind.

1924: What Was Happening?

Howard Carter discovered the sarcophagus of Tutankhamen. Stanley Baldwin's government fell, and he was replaced by Ramsay MacDonald at the head of Britain's first Labour government, only for that too to fall and for Baldwin to resume as PM by the end of the same year. The British Empire Exhibition opened at Wembley. France hosted the first Winter Olympic Games. The Ford Motor Company manufactured its ten millionth Model T. Britain signed a trade agreement with Germany while, in time for Christmas, the unknown Adolf Hitler was released early from a German jail.

What was the Good Cause?

War had ended in 1918 but, in the decade that followed, wounds had not healed. Many families still grieved their lost ones, while many who had served their country and survived found that the country they had fought for had now moved on. Jobs and houses were hard to find – harder still for those wounded in the war. In the country which had said 'We will not forget', some people *had* forgotten. But the **British Legion** had not.

The annual **Poppy Appeal** makes the British Legion one of the best-known charities working in Britain today. Founded three years after the First World War, the charity held its first Poppy Appeal that year (1921) on the anniversary of Armistice Day – though it wasn't until the following year that the famous poppies began to be made by disabled soldiers themselves (members of the newly-formed Disabled Society).

Three years later the charity issued the British Legion Album.

THE
BRITISH LEGION
ALBUM

IN AID OF FIELD-MARSHAL
EARL HAIG'S APPEAL
FOR EX-SERVICE MEN OF ALL RANKS

THE BRITISH LEGION ALBUM

In Aid Of Field-Marshal Earl Haig's Appeal For Ex-Servicemen Of All Ranks
published in 1924 by Cassell and Company Ltd
Main pages unnumbered, plus 36 pages of advertisements, all 22.5cm x 28.5cm
Green & buff card covers, both with a pasted-on coloured plate

Different in look and conception to the wartime Gift Books, and stronger than one might expect from a book produced like an oversize paperback, this book gains interest from close perusal. Many of its pages comprise little more – sometimes nothing more – than facsimile signatures. But the book holds around twenty illustrations and many snippets of text from the famous of their day. Readers in the 1920s would have found it interesting to see examples of their actual handwriting, and for us today it is still intriguing to have those distant names recalled and reanimated on the page.

Haig himself writes a double-spread Foreword, speaking, he says, '*for the ex-servicemen of the British Legion, to whose benefit will be devoted whatever money this unique collection of autographs may bring in.*

It is more than a '*mere assemblage of famous signatures,*' he continues, in his clear hand: '*Each signature is an acknowledgement of the simplest and grandest of human virtues; the love of liberty and fair dealing among men, courage, patriotism and self-sacrifice. All whose names are found within these pages have shown by their readiness to help living ex-service men, the depth and the sincerity of their respect, and gratitude, towards the dead; towards fallen comrades of ours, who dying left homes and dear ones destitute; towards the gallant lads who fell on the threshold of life.'*

The Queen takes the following page (*'It gives me great pleasure . . . '*) and other members of the royal family add their names to the next four pages. Princess Alice, President of the Women's Section of the British Legion, writes that the Appeal *'should meet with a particularly eager response from the Women of the Empire, for they owe everything to those gallant men who answered the call of duty, not counting the cost.'* Asquith and Lloyd George follow, with a page each, as has Robert Baden Powell – and notables crowd the following pages.

The example of sense of Duty and of self-sacrifice for their country, as set by the men of the British Legion in the Great War, is not one that should be allowed to die.

It is our aim, therefore, in the Boy Scout movement to keep it alive in the next generation by holding up the ideal and encouraging its pursuit among the Scouts

Robert Baden-Powell

Many pages comprise groups of like names, each listed more legibly alongside to explain the signatures. Thus we have a page from the Royal Family (Albert, Elizabeth, Henry, George . . .); three pages from His Majesty's Household; a page each from France, Italy, Spain, America and Belgium; two pages of heroes. Other groupings include members of the Cabinet, the House of Lords and House of Commons; attendees at the Imperial Conference, 1923; writers, actors, artists, distinguished doctors, scientists, Leaders of Religion, judges and barristers, London Newspaper Proprietors, 'A Fleet Street Page' and one from 'The Provincial Press', nurses, members of the Shackleton-Powett Expedition and the 1922 Everest Expedition, some cricketers and, of course, Leaders of His Majesty's Forces. Three pages of signatures come from 'Some Notable Women'.

Sheila Kaye-Smith gives an extract from 'Little England'; Sir Philip Gibbs writes 'After the Cease Fire!'; and there are extracts in their own hand from works by Conrad, Gosse, Belloc, Rider Haggard, John Buchan, Arnold Bennett, Galsworthy, Marjorie Bowen, A A Milne, Eden Phillpotts, George Moore, Chesterton, Shaw and others. Robert Bridges provides a poem ('Of the first B.E.F.'); other poems come from Walter de la Mare, Yeats (whose 'Innisfree' would be illegible were it not that most readers knew the poem), May Sinclair, John Drinkwater, Arthur Symons, Maurice Hewlett, Owen Seaman, Sir Henry Newbolt and more.

Conan Doyle tells us that '*The system which left seven million dead upon the fields of Europe must be rotten to the core. Time will elapse before the true message is mastered but when that day arrives the war of 1914 may be regarded as the end of the dark ages and the start of that upward path which leads away from personal or national selfishness towards the City Beautiful upon the distant hills.*'

Sir Herbert Hughes-Stanton supplies an attractive watercolour frontispiece, showing the deceptively peaceful little town of Albert, 1917. Princess Louise, Duchess of Argyle, a noted artist, gives a wistful full-page 'Remembrance' portrait. H M Bateman and comedian George Robey give playful self-portraits. William Rothenstein, John Hassall, William Orpen, Augustus John, W Heath Robinson, C R W Nevinson, Solomon J Solomon, D Y Cameron, Frank Short, John Collier, W L Wyllie, Chaliapine, Tom Webster add further pictures.

William Orpen's contribution

Celebrated composers (including Paderewski, Holst, Bax, Elgar, Ireland, Vaughan Williams, Walford Davies, Henry Wood, Sir Thomas Beecham, Coates, Goossens, Josef Holbrooke, Roger Quilter, Sir Landon Ronald and Ravel) jot down scraps of their music. The singer Tetrazzini, known for rarely giving autographs, gives one here – as does Nellie Melba and Clara Butt. Dame Ethel Smyth, typically if surprisingly for such a patriotic volume, sets to music the line 'Men are fools that wish to die'. Puccini scrawls two bars from 'Madame Butterfly' across a page.

The main text ends with a handwritten extract from Ian Hay's wartime hit *The First Hundred Thousand*, which begins: '*We shall win this war one day, and most of the credit will go, as usual, to those who are in at the finish. But – when we assign the glory and the praise, let us not forget those who stood up to the first rush.*' As his text concludes: '*Let us bare our heads to the memory of those battered, decimated, indomitable legions who saved us from utter extinction at the beginning.*' Facing his page is the first of 38 pages (including the back cover) of advertisements contributing to the Fund. These alone are nostalgic reading, coming from firms like *Punch* magazine, Lifebuoy Soap, Ovaltine, Marconiphone, Underwood typewriters, Kodak (A "Kodak" never forgets!), Johnnie Walker, Eno's Fruit Salt, Jeyes, The British Commercial Gas Association, Colman's Mustard ('Try it in your bath . . . '), Swan Fountpens [sic], the Bibby Line, Stanley Gibbons, Bean Cars (whatever happened to them?), BL Scotch Whisky – at 15/- per bottle and at 'pre-war quality and strength', the Atco Motor Mower, Gillette ('The shave with the smile in it!'), Horrockses Nainsooks, Cambrics & Madapolams ('They have been famous for over a century – your guarantee of enduring worth'), Boots the Chemists, Phosferine and, in pride of place on the outside back cover, Players Navy Cut tobacco ("Leading the way").

This family is perhaps the target market advertised to in the
British Legion Album

Perhaps the most touching contribution comes from 'the late Frederic Harrison, written on Armistice Day, 1922, in his 91st year'. In shaky handwriting, it begins: '*A father whose elder son was from 1914 to 1919 staff officer in the French, and then in the British, Army, whose younger son fell in battle at Festubert in 1915, appeals to English men and women to help all service men to enjoy a fitting life at home.*'

103

1929: What Was Happening?

In America, Chicago experienced the St Valentine's Day Massacre, in which seven gangsters were killed. The Wall Street Stock Market crashed (not for that reason), bringing about a worldwide recession and ultimately, the Great Depression while, in New York, Cole Porter premiered his new musical *Wake Up and Dream*. Here in Britain, Ramsay MacDonald formed a minority Labour government. The French government fell. In Italy, Mussolini's Fascist government banned the use of foreign words.

What was the Good Cause?
Successful as the *British Legion Album* was in raising funds, the book could not compare with the **Poppy Appeal**, which was successful from the outset and has since grown until it has become a several-week annual fund-raising campaign, climaxing on November 11th every year. That day, Armistice Day, is for civilians the most visible reminder of the British Legion and the work it does. But the Legion (which since 1971 has been called the *Royal* British Legion) works *throughout* the year to support those who have served or are still serving in the Forces.

Although it is associated in many people's minds principally with the two world wars, the charity's work extends to help ex-Service personnel and families affected by all conflicts, large and small – not just those from the past but, sadly, those continuing today. The charity also maintains the National Memorial Arboretum in Staffordshire.

Five years after the publication of *The British Legion Album* came its successor, *The Legion Book*.

THE LEGION BOOK

edited by Captain H Cotton Minchin
published in September 1929 by Cassell and Company
Ltd.
234 pages plus 14 prelims, 22.5cm x 29cm,
maroon cloth-bound cover, spine blocked in gold

Not to be confused with *The British Legion Album*
published 5 years earlier, the format of this book has
more in common with rival publisher Hodder and
Stoughton Gift Books although, published a decade after
the war and by a different firm, the genre has moved on.
Gone are the tipped-in coloured plates, although this
book is well illustrated, gone are the facsimile
signatures, and gone is the war-soaked tone. Though the
British Legion was the recipient, it is not even made
clear where the profits will go, despite an
acknowledgement to 'Captain Willcox, MBE, of British
Legion Headquarters' (among others). The Editor's
Note merely states that book is published 'due to the
personal interest of HRH The Prince of Wales, at whose
invitation the contributors were pleased to come
forward.'

The book was a runaway success, with six editions
between September and December of 1929 alone –
perhaps because the contributions seemed less high-
minded and more readable than in some earlier books.
The opening short story by Hugh Walpole turned out to
be the first chapter of an abandoned novel (in earlier Gift
Books he had also sent in extracts rather than stand-
alone contributions), and he was followed by Margaret
Kennedy, A E Coppard, Storm Jameson, Sarah Gertrude
Millin, Rebecca West, Sapper and P G Wodehouse
(whose title, 'Disentangling Old Percy' will have
delighted some old soldiers). Biographical fragments

came from John Galsworthy, Winston Churchill (writing on Haig), David Garnett, Edmund Blunden and F Tennyson Jesse, whose 'Caribbean Waters' was illustrated by Edward Bawden.

Edgar Wallace wrote a piece on the eternal British soldier, Thomas Atkins. Arnold Bennett gave 'Debtors Who Have Short Memories', in which he ticked off British civilians who had forgotten all too soon their returning soldiers. Hilaire Belloc wrote two pages 'On Prophets', rather cheekily ending his short piece by saying, 'But really, when it comes to prophecies that fail, one could fill a book, and I've written enough already.' Sheila Kaye-Smith told of 'Sussex Revisited'. Poems run through the pages from Rudyard Kipling, Robert Bridges, Laurence Binyon, Aldous Huxley, Henry Newbolt, J C Squire, John Drinkwater, Gilbert Murray (giving an unilluminating translation of Theocritus), G K Chesterton (with a similarly closed-in 'To St Michael, in Time of Peace'), Walter de la Mare (just as unclear with 'The Image'), Humbert Wolfe, W H Davies, Bliss Carman and Vita Sackville-West. Edith Sitwell provides the Scotch Rhapsody from 'Facade', and Reginald Berkeley closes the book with a racially off-colour playlet entitled 'The Prince Consort' which will not nowadays be performed.

Doctor Faustus Conjuring Mephostophilis
by *Eric Ravilious*

Royal portraits are presented by Sir Arthur Cope, Sir William Llewellyn and William Rothenstein, while Admiral Jellicoe is drawn by Oswald Birley. Max Beerbohm caricatures eleven prime ministers on one page. More conventional full-page illustrations come from A K Lawrence (a sexy 'Study for Head of Persephone'), James McBey, John Sargent (sketches for his monumental 'Gassed'), Eric Kennington, Augustus John and Jacob Epstein, while Eric Ravilious and Clare Leighton provide striking woodcuts ('Doctor Faustus' from Ravilious, and 'Snow Shovellers' from Leighton). Cartoons come from the pen of 'Strube' (*Daily Express* cartoonist Sidney Conrad Strube) and 'Poy' (P H Fearon), while David Low gives a page of portrait drawings from his sketch book.

107

TRIOLET, BY POY.

We have filled up this space,
Nothing else are we doing.
We have come to this place,
And are posing with grace;
We have rolled up in case
Nothing else was ensuing.
We have filled up this space,
Nothing else are we doing!

A Triolet, by Poy (P. H. Fearon)

108

1935: What Was Happening?

The Thirties made a troubled decade. The Great Crash had been followed by the Great Depression and, while millions were thrown out of work, a small but rich minority sought to create a decade of style. Hitler was in power in Germany. Mussolini continued to head his Italian Fascist government, Spain was a dictatorship, and even democratic Britain had some two or three million Fascist supporters. There were riots in the streets.

King George V died. Edward VIII took the crown. Few realized for how short a time.

What was the Good Cause?

The Princess Elizabeth of York Hospital for Children

The East London Hospital for Children (the first in London to take children under two years old) had begun its life in a converted warehouse at Ratcliff Cross in 1868, having been established after the 1866 Cholera outbreak by the paediatrician Dr Nathaniel Heckford and his vigorous wife Sarah. Heckford died tragically young of consumption in 1871. The hospital was described in December 1868 by Dickens in his essay, 'A Small Star in the East'. Dickens, perhaps unsurprisingly, noted that 'insufficient food and unwholesome living are the most frequent causes of disease among the small patients.' In 1875 the hospital moved to a new building in Shadwell, when it became known as the Shadwell Hospital for Women and Children, later renamed the East London Hospital For Children And Dispensary For Women.

In 1932 it became the Princess Elizabeth of York Hospital for Children – the young Princess Elizabeth, as future heir to the throne and, as we now know, Britain's longest-serving monarch, being much in the newspapers of the day. Ten years later, in 1942, the hospital was amalgamated with The Queen's Hospital for Children in Hackney, to become The Queen Elizabeth Hospital for Children, and by 1945 it had over 200 beds. The hospital continued to function on two sites: Queen Elizabeth, Hackney Road and Queen Elizabeth, Shadwell. A third site at Banstead, Surrey – the Banstead Wood Country Hospital – was opened in 1948, but by the early 1960s there were less than 50 beds at Shadwell, and the hospital closed in 1963. It is now one of several merged into The Barts and The London NHS Trust. Others in that Trust include the Queen Elizabeth Hospital for Children, The Royal London and St Bartholomew's.

The PRINCESS ELIZABETH GIFT BOOK

In aid of the Princess Elizabeth of York Hospital for Children
Published in 1935 by Hodder & Stoughton
224 pages, 18.5cm x 25cm, cream cloth-bound cover blocked in dark blue

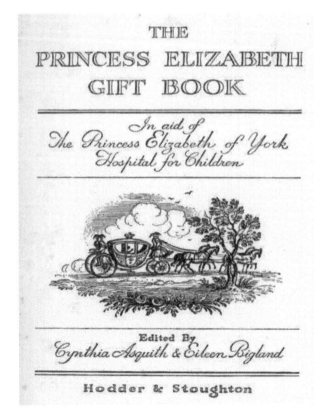

The traditions of First World War Gift Books are both retained and updated in this attractive volume, edited by Cynthia Asquith and Eileen Bigland. The colour plates are no longer tipped-in and although they still occupy a full page they come from competent but less prestigious artists. Rex Whistler's baroque end-papers contrast with a formal frontispiece of the young princess by society painter Laszlo, opening cartoons by Bip Pares and 2 double-page spreads from the Disney studios of *Mickey Mouse and His Retinue Arriving at the Party* and *The End of the Party: Mickey Mouse takes a Photograph*. The book is introduced 'from the children in the Princess Elizabeth Hospital' as an invitation to 'all the people and animals we loved to read about to come to a party and tell us their adventures', and a mock invitation card to the party appears on page 9. A particularly good idea is to supply a double-page spread of photographs showing how each contributor looked when young.

'Uncle Oojah's Little Princess' by H M Talintyre

If other artists are not of the very top rank, they certainly are well chosen for a book designed for children's enjoyment: Paul Bloomfield, A B Payne (illustrator for the *Daily Mirror* cartoon 'Pip, Squeak and Wilfred'), Sylvia Salisbury, Mary Tourtel (creator of Rupert), A H Watson, Herbert S Foxwell (visualiser of Teddy Tail), L R Brightwell (for the Hepzibah Hen illustrations), Laurian Jones ('when she was eight years old'), H M Talintyre (illustrator for Uncle Oojah) and, of course, the Disney Studios and Bip Pares.

'Hepzibah Hen' by L R Brightwell

The writers are more famous: J M Barrie (with a cloying 'A Children's Hospital in War Time'), Rudyard Kipling (a Just-So story), Francis Brett Young (a natural history lesson wrapped up in a story), G K Chesterton (a typically ironic poem that will have been above most children's heads), B J Lamb ('Uncle Dick' of the *Daily Mirror*, beside a 4-page cartoon of Pip, Squeak and Wilfred), Algernon Blackwood (giving a dog's-eye view of the Coronation), Jan Struther (the creator of Mrs Miniver and, in the First World War, the organizer of Camp Libraries for the troops, who gives a poem about 'Princess Jane of London Town'), Mary Tourtel (writing and illustrating a Rupert story), Compton Mackenzie ('The Fairy Washerwoman'), Herbert Asquith (providing a poem from the son of a previous Prime Minister and being the husband of this book's editor).

Elizabeth Bowen is a surprising choice and supplies an uncharacteristic fairy story, 'The Unromantic Princess: '*When the Princess was born the Queen, who knew what was usual, invited two Fairy Godmothers to her christening. Unfortunately, they arrived in a workaday mood, and full of modern ideas about girls. . .* ' James Hilton follows with 'an episode in the life of Mr Chips' (about schooldays); Walter de la Mare's poem, 'Stars', is one few children would have liked; Margaret Irwin, a trades unionist and Fabian activist, gives 'an historical play in one act', which ditto. Then comes W H Davies (a hand-written poem, 'Street Cries'), Shirley Cooke ('Woolly Bear's Aeroplane'), Lord David Cecil (the historian and literary critic, another of the editor's friends, with a poem, 'A Sixteenth Century Princess Elizabeth at Hatfield'), Una L Lascot ('Teddy Tail's Circus'), Olwen Bowen (a Hepzibah Hen story), L A G Strong (an odd tale of a seagull helping out at harvest time), Denis Mackail ('The Story of Rather Greedy Little Hugh'), Enid Bagnold (author of *National Velvet*, with the very different 'Putting Tucker to Bed'), Flo Lancaster ('Uncle Oojah's Little Princess'), Hugh Walpole (a reminiscence of 'The Little Chair with the Gold Tread') and John Drinkwater (with the concluding poem, 'For A Princess'):

Princess, at nine you've taken
A people for your friend,
Let love be so unshaken
Until your journey's end.

Long before that journey's end the Princess, of course, would become Queen Elizabeth the Second.

1939: What Was Happening?

1939 was a nervous year. An earthquake in Chile killed 30,000, and more died later in the aftershock. In Europe few people reacted, as most Europeans were more worried about war –war with Germany – which had been expected the previous year (1938) when, after five years of Hitler's rule, Germany invaded Czechoslovakia. Yet somehow a war which had seemed inevitable had been avoided, though not before Britain had put in place preparations for conflict and had practiced evacuation from its cities and vulnerable areas. Was war still inevitable? Most people thought so, despite Prime Minister Chamberlain having promised 'Peace in our time' and although until August 1939 the *Daily Express* stoutly maintained 'There will be no war in Europe this year or next'. War was declared on September the 3rd.

What was the Good Cause?
St Bartholomew's

The country's oldest surviving hospital, founded in the reign of Henry I, was an imposing stone building in West Smithfield, standing between Christ's Hospital and Smithfield on the site of the ancient priory of St. Bartholomew, and its western gate looked out onto the stone-paved and noisy neighbourhood of the London Central Meat Market. Since the 18th century it had run its own medical school (male students only till 1947, with the one exception – presumably regretted – of Elizabeth Blackwell nearly a hundred years before), and it had founded its own nursing school in 1877. As a walk-in general hospital serving Londoners rich and poor, Barts was always respected and much loved (Hogarth's paintings to the main staircase were given free).

In the First World War the hospital would tend some 5,400 wounded soldiers. Not surprisingly, fund-raisers at the time forbore to mention that the hospital also contained its own 'German Hospital', originally founded 'for the reception of all poor Germans and others speaking the German language', principally the many German immigrants in London. (In the 19th century Germans had been by far the largest immigrant community.) Throughout those years the hospital had had active support from the German royal family and in the Great War, despite strong anti-German feelings in Britain and a shortage of nurses and doctors in Germany, some German staff remained at the Hospital. The German Hospital continued at Barts till 1987, when it transferred to the new Homerton Hospital.

ROSE WINDOW

A tribute offered to St. Bartholomew's Hospital by Twenty-Five Authors
With a foreword by The Lord Horder GCVO, MD, FRCP

Published by William Heinemann Ltd in 1939
385 pages, 22½ cm x 29½ cm, red cloth-bound cover

Issued just before the Second World War, this is a mixed bag of submissions from 12 authors and 10 poets, with 3 specially written playlets, the whole enhanced with fine illustrations in black and white throughout by Anna Zinkeisen. (Two examples are shown here.) Short stories come from Marjorie Bowen, Vera Brittain, Eric Linklater, A G MacDonell and others, and they vie with extracts from what were then unpublished novels from J B Priestley and Hugh Walpole. Priestley's *Prologue to*

an Unfinished Novel is just that, a typically whimsical but readable episode in which the mild Mr Filey, recovering from some kind of mental breakdown, finds himself sharing a railway carriage with a man who appears to be a murderer on the run. The novel, one suspects, was 'unfinished' because it had nowhere to run, and contrasts with Hugh Walpole's submission of a chapter from his *Bright Pavilions* 'which may possibly be published in the autumn of 1940' and which was to become the first of his 'Herries Saga.'

A typically powerful Zinkeisen illustration

It's worth the trying. For to tend and heal
The sick with all the power our times afford
Is a creed to us, a thing we feel
Is something mightier than Achilles' sword.

From For St. Bartholomew's by Lord Dunsany

A contrast in characters:

2 studies from Rose Window
drawn by Anna Zinkeisen for *The Last of Casanova*
A Comedy in One Act
By George R. Preedy

Dominique Stetzl,
Steward to Graf Waldstein
Stetzl, the Major-Domo of the Estate:
a rather pompous man of middle age, well set up,
in knee-breeches and powder.

Giacomo Casanova

*The screen is moved and CASANOVA
appears; he is wrapped in a gold and
scarlet mantle, wears his own hair; all
signs of old age have disappeared. He is
young, proud and gay. TERESA shrinks
against the desk.*

1939 . . . Two Great London Causes

The Lord Mayor of London's Fund
The Lord Mayor's Appeal, an annual affair capable of touching some very well-filled bank accounts, asked every year for donations from smaller wallets also, those of ordinary people, principally but not exclusively Londoners. Earlier in 1939 the Lord Mayor's Fund had set about raising money to rebuild St Bartholomew's Hospital. Now, with the Second World War begun, the appeal's target was expanded from a single London hospital to both the Red Cross internationally and the worldwide health and religious charity, the Order of St John of Jerusalem.

The Order of St John of Jerusalem
The charity chosen by the Lord Mayor of London in 1939 to benefit from funds raised by *The Queen's Book of the Red Cross* is a largely medical charity. It still runs today; one of its current two key objects is: "The encouragement and promotion of all work of humanity and charity for the relief of persons in sickness, distress, suffering or danger, without distinction of race, class or creed and the extension of the second great principle of the Order embodied in the Motto 'Pro Utilitate Hominum'." Its other key object is unequivocal: "The encouragement of all that makes for the spiritual and moral strengthening of mankind in accordance with the first great principle of the Order embodied in the Motto 'Pro Fide'."

The charity was founded in the 11th century, earned its royal charter from Queen Victoria in 1888 and nowadays works in some 40 countries, having a salaried staff of around 4,000.

'The Red Cross of Comfort' by J Morton Sale

THE QUEEN'S BOOK OF THE RED CROSS

With a message from Her Majesty the Queen
And Contributions from Fifty British Authors and Artists
in Aid of The Lord Mayor of London's Fund for the Red
Cross
and the Order of St John of Jerusalem

Published in November 1939 by Hodder and Stoughton
18.5cm x 25cm, blue cloth-bound cover blocked in red

The Queen was Elizabeth, wife of King George V and known as such, rather than as Elizabeth II (a title her daughter would acquire later). Her opening message, in facsimile handwriting on Buckingham Palace notepaper, concludes: '*All you who buy my book, as well as the distinguished authors and artists who prepared it, are helping forward the great work of mercy on the battlefield; to all of you I would send this Christmas message – God bless you. Elizabeth R.*' The publishers, in a note opposite, express gratitude to the contributors whose cooperation made it possible for the book to be produced within two months of its conception (two months, therefore, after the start of the war).

AUGUST 1939
The Evacuation of School Children was
carried out with complete success.

'The Evacuation of Schoolchildren was Carried Out with
Complete Success' by Mabel Lucie Attwell

Short stories in the book comprise A E W
Mason's 'The Conjuror', Ian Hay's 'The Man Who Had
Something Against Him', D L Murray's 'Only a Sojer!',
H M Tomlinson's 'Ports of Call', Daphne du Maurier's
'The Escort', Jan Struther's 'Mrs Miniver Makes a List',
Eric Ambler's 'The Army of the Shadows', Humfrey
Jordan's 'The Boatswain Yawned', Lady Olive
Douglas's 'Such an Odd War!', Howard Spring's

'Christmas Honeymoon', Dorothy Whipple's 'No Robbery', Lord Mottistone's reminiscence 'Tell Them, Warrior', L A G Strong's 'A Gift from Christy Keogh', Denis Mackail's 'It's the Thought that Counts', Georgette Heyer's 'Pursuit', H C Bailey's Mr Fortune story 'The Thistle Down' and Ruby Ferguson's 'Mrs Memmary's Visitors'.

Poems come from John Masefield ('Red Cross'), T S Eliot ('The Marching Song of the Pollicle Dogs' and 'Billy M'Caw: the Remarkable Parrot'), Alfred Noyes ('A Child's Gallop' and 'The Stranger') and a final two from Walter de la Mare ('And So To Bed' and 'Joy'). Hugh Walpole, as ever with his Gift Book contributions, submits an extract from one of his books (*The Herries Chronicle*). Charles Morgan supplies a thoughtful discourse on 'Creative Imagination' while Howard Marshall pictures 'The Fisherman's England'. Cecil Roberts takes the reader 'Down Ferry Lane', Ann Bridge recollects the 1935 Jubilee, Gracie Fields provides an unexpected thought 'On Getting Better' after her recent well-publicised illness, and C H Middleton, gardening journalist, tells us to 'Keep That Garden Going'.

Mary Thomas gives hints and diagrams on knitting, while Frank S Smythe climbs the mountains in 'The Crag'. Cecil Hardwicke and Edith Evans write on the theatre, A A Milne contributes a duologue, while Ivor Novello supplies the words and music to 'We'll Remember'. J B Morton pens a comic lyric 'for bagpipes and twelve hundred and forty voices', while C Day Lewis provides intellectual stimulus with a translation from Virgil's Georgics. Collie Knox rounds off the book with an oddly-typeset autobiographic piece on the Red Cross, entitled 'This Flag Still Flies Over all Mankind'.

This volume contains less illustrations than in

127

similar Gift Books, though they are from noted artists. In contrast to those other Gift Books, most of the works look to the symbolic rather than the real. Russell Flint decorates some words from the King, Edmund Dulac startles the reader with a symbolic battle 'twixt good and evil, while Frank Brangwyn provides a less startling piece of symbolism in a black and white sketch of God comforting a wounded soldier. Bip Pares submits a more formal piece of symbolism (representing Faith at the bed of death), while Arthur Wragg provides one of his stark black and white religious cuts.

Rex Whistler contributes his own symbolic painting, 'In The Wilderness':

Elsewhere, Edmund Blampied's sketch, 'The Symbol' looks forward to a Christian victory on the battlefield, while Morton Sale's sketch, 'The Red Cross of Comfort', stays just this side of sentimentality. Symbolism is eschewed by the remaining three artists: Laura Knight draws some 'Hop Pickers', Mabel Lucie Attwell over-sweetens a study of a sleepy evacuee (shown above), and Norman Wilkinson paints a stormy sea above the words '*Outside the storms of war may blow and the land may be lashed with the fury of its gales, but in our own hearts . . . there is peace.*'

1944: What Was happening?

By 1944 the outcome of the war had long seemed inevitable: Germany had lost but would not accept defeat. On its Eastern Front Germany faced its one-time ally Russia, and on its Western Front the British and Colonial forces had been joined by American troops. The prospect and near certainty of defeat only made Germany fight harder. The Allied countries continued to face heavy losses on the home front as well as on the battlefields while within those beleaguered home fronts the people, saddened by the death of loved ones and weakened by shortages of all kinds, tried to return to something approaching real life.

What was the Cause?

The Hospital for Women, Soho

Reputed to be the first hospital in London for the 'treatment of those maladies which neither rank, nor wealth, nor character can avert from the female sex', the Hospital for Women began in Red Lion Square in 1844 and moved to 30 Soho Square in 1852, expanding into number 29 in 1865 and taking numbers 3 and 4 Frith Street into the main building in the 20th century. It was now a striking prominence, with matt glazed white faience and stucco façade, dormered green slate mansard and a parapet inscribed with the words 'The Hospital for Women'. Numbers 5 to 7 Frith Street were acquired in 1914 and 1924, and a new private ward for paying patients was opened in 1925. On the outbreak of the Second World War in 1939 the hospital was closed and a First Aid Post opened in the Outpatients Department, but in June the following year the hospital was partially reopened. The hospital took control of the First Aid Post from Westminster City Council, who continued to fund it.

In 1944, when *Soho Centenary* was published, John Laver's Foreword could end with optimistic confidence: '*The hospital has gone on expanding ever since, and is now so linked with the fortunes of Soho that it is impossible to imagine it away, even if anybody wished to do so. May it long continue to form a part of the old and honourable district in which it has made its home.*' Yet within two years it had gone. In 1946 the Hospital made plans to merge with the Samaritan Free Hospital but the idea was abandoned when, on the establishment of the National Health Service in 1948, the Hospital for Women became part of The Middlesex Hospital Group. In 1988 it merged with the Elizabeth Garrett Anderson Hospital in Euston Road. The building is now The Soho Centre – a walk-in clinic providing health information, advice and treatment for minor illnesses and injuries for people who live, work in or are visiting the area.

SOHO CENTENARY

Dedicated to Her Majesty Queen Mary,
Patroness since 1901 of the Hospital for Women, Soho
Square, W.1.
published for Christmas in 1944 by Hutchinson & Co,
Ltd.
108 pages, 18.5cm x 25cm, stone coloured board cover,
blocked in gold

frontispiece by Eric Kennington

This wartime volume is inevitably less lavish than its
forbears but still manages to attract writings and
illustrations of good quality – it is, as the title page
declares, 'A Gift from Artists, Writers and Musicians to
the Soho Hospital for Women'. In 1944 the hospital
reached its centenary, having been founded in Red Lion

Square in 1844, before transferring to Soho Square 8 years later. Soho, '*that little square which lies just south of Oxford Street and west of Charing Cross Road*', as James Laver's Foreword explains, gained its name from '*the shout of the citizens of London when they hunted the hare over what were then open fields; it was the battle cry of Monmouth's soldiers as they rallied for the last desperate charge at Sedgemoor.*' Monmouth's connection comes from his building himself a house in 1681 on the south side of what is now Soho Square (the land was his). By 1720 the Square was flanked by elegant houses. Monmouth's house was demolished in 1773, and it was to that site that the Hospital for Women transferred in 1852.

A Peter Cheyney *femme fatale* drawn by Anna Zinkeisen

Inside the book we find stories from Mary Lavin, Marguerite Steen, Roland Pertwee, I A R Wylie, F Tennyson Jesse, Noel Streatfeild, E L Almedingen and thriller-writer Peter Cheyney.   Poems are contributed by John Masefield, Clemence Dane, John Jarmain (who was killed in action in June 1944), Virginia Graham, Robert Nichols and John Pudney. Short essays come from Elizabeth Bowen (a particularly interesting piece on what was a common wartime phenomenon, calico windows – installed after a glass-destroying blast), Doctor Tancred Borenius (giving an unexpected piece on Walter Sickert), Charles Cochran the impresario, Margaret Lane, A H McIndoe (on disabled soldiers), Storm Jameson (discussing how France *will* survive the war), G B Stern (on R L Stevenson), Frank Swinnerton (on his lifelong task of reviewing), Michael Balcon (on humorists), Emlyn Williams (whose 'Portrait of a Londoner' has her say, '*That 'Itler, dropping bombs on Reg and me an' such . . . you know, 'e's a bad loser.*').

Stephen Vincent Benét supplies a verse drama ('A Child Is Born') and Hubert Foss presents a piece on music relating to Soho, illustrated with examples of handwritten sheets.

Illustrations are a mixture of black & white and coloured plates, plus some effective in-text drawings from Anna Zinkeisen. Eric Kennington provides the coloured frontispiece, and other coloured plates come from Sir William Nicholson, C R W Nevinson, R O Dunlop and Anna Zinkeisen again. Black & white plates come from George Belcher, John Cole, Steven Spurrier, Anna Zinkeisen, her sister Doris (twice), Bernard Adams, H Rushbury, Robert Greenham, Charles Pears, C F Tunnicliffe and Hamzah Carr.

Lacking the righteous patriotism of the First World War Gift Books, this more modest volume conveys its own 1940s war spirit, more sombre, more reflective, more self-aware.

1945: What Was happening?

At long last the war was over. But the hoarse jubilation of crowds soon gave way to the realities of rationing: shortages were more severe now than they had been in wartime; families were painfully reunited and regrouped. A Labour government swept to power – ousting Churchill, the seemingly impregnable war leader and, so people hoped, ousting the social evils of the old guard.

War damage was all about, and many bomb sites would not be cleared for another decade. No one had any money and neither, people found, had the government: all the money had been spent and the country was in debt.

To the victors had been awarded an empty cup.

What was the Cause?
Saint Mary's Hospitals for Women and Children, Manchester
Saint Mary's Hospital was founded in 1790 by Dr Charles White and, over the years, the hospital developed a wide range of world-class medical services for women, babies and children as well as a comprehensive Genetics Centre and an internationally recognised teaching and research portfolio. From 1855 to 1903 it occupied a new building in Quay Street, erected at the expense of another doctor, Thomas Radford. Then, in 1904, it was amalgamated with the Manchester Southern Hospital for Women and Children, following which two new hospitals were built, one in Whitworth Street West on the corner of Oxford Street, and the other on Oxford Road in Chorlton on Medlock. More recently, in 2009, paediatric (but not neonatal) services from St Mary's Hospital were transferred to the new Royal Manchester Children's Hospital.

In 1945 its funds were low.

VOICES ON THE GREEN

A Gift Book on behalf of St Mary's Hospitals
Published by Michael Joseph Ltd in December 1945,
shortly after the Second Word War ended.
324 pages, 22cm x 28½ cm, beige cloth-bound cover

As this was a book in aid of a Hospital for Women and
Children the editors chose, rather than begin with a
'Foreword' or 'Introduction', to give a 2-page 'Pre-
Natal', in which they made it clear that:

> *Although the profits are to be devoted to
> the funds of these hospitals the primary
> purpose of the book is to deepen and
> spread a general appreciation of the
> needs of mothers and children, and of the
> family as a unit of society. The authors
> and artists whose contributions appear in
> the book will not necessarily address
> themselves directly to this theme; our
> suggestion is that, submitting themselves
> to its inspiration, they should contribute
> some piece of their own kind of creative
> work—whether it be verse, a story or an
> essay lightly celebrating some chosen
> aspect or treating some problem of social
> life for which the writer feels particular
> concern. We picture the cumulative whole
> as an artistic unity, a little loosely held
> together perhaps, but rich in variety of
> substance and manner and sharing the
> same broad inspiration ...*

'Snow on the Radnor Hills' by Iain Macnab

A late entry to the Gift Book stakes, modest in format
and now quite hard to find, *Voices On The Green* is one
of the better anthologies, containing 38 pieces from
leading authors and graced with 11 full-page engravings
and over 20 black and white vignettes from top artists of
the day – including Blair Hughes-Stanton, Eric
Ravilious, Guy Malet, Agnes Miller Parker, Iain
MacNab, Robert Gibbings, Claire Leighton and Clifford
Webb. Though printed on wartime economy paper, the
book is worth seeking out for the illustrations alone.
Authors include H E Bates, Edmund Blunden, Marjorie
Bowen, James Bridie, Vera Brittain, John Brophy,
Walter de la Mare, Walter Greenwood, A P Herbert,

138

Ethel Mannin, Viola Meynell, J B Priestley, Roger Quilter, Vita Sackville-West, Stephen Spender, Howard Spring and Henry Williamson. The book is edited by A R J Wise and Reginald A Smith.

The epilogue reminds us of how Britain's health was cared for shortly before the new Labour Government's installation of a National Health Service – but continues:

'The Hospital has plans for the future, it is pledged to go forward—and this means money; and money given freely by those who believe that there is a margin of individual enterprise and free pioneer spirit wherein lies the value of a voluntary hospital. There are beds to be endowed – names to be remembered immortally. Will you add a page to this book by sending a gift according to your ability to the Honorary Treasurer, Saint Mary's Hospitals, Manchester, 13.'

'The Hansom Cab' by Eric Ravilious

CONTRIBUTORS
– Who *Were* These People?

an Anna Zinkeisen sketch for 'On Letter-Writing' in *Rose Window*

Gift Books of the Edwardian age, then of the First World War, then on into the Thirties, were designed to be impressive coffee-table books, with lavish illustrations accompanied by equally prestigious words. (Paper shortages and government restrictions put an end to that in the Second World War.) The finest authors and poets would be used alongside celebrities and notables of the day. Often, the writers would *sign* their work; facsimile signatures adding to the perceived value of the books – as indeed they do. Even today there is a small thrill to be gained from seeing, scratched across the page, the actual handwriting of long-dead famous names.

Who would have thought that Queen Alexandra's handwriting would be so pronouncedly untidy, or that the flamboyant poet Yeats wrote in such a crabbed unreadable hand? Arnold Bennett is similarly unreadable – as indeed are the lines from a good many brought up, we were led to believe, in an age of rigid copper-plate. Shaw's is that of a pernickety old man, Chesterton's strong and a little fancy. The poet Arthur Symons, having written out his poem 'Japan', submits his copy defaced with a splatter of ink across the final verse. Is this not interesting to see? Would you not have liked the chance, on succeeding pages, to compare the handwriting of your two Prime Ministers, W H Asquith and Lloyd George? (Baldwin is there also.)

We must remember that, to the readers of Gift Books, these were people they knew, albeit remotely and second-hand. So to have a writer's entry signed off personally added weight to even the most cursory contribution. A few *were* cursory; writers like Hugh Walpole and H G Wells tossed in old work (an 1890s story from Wells, work in progress from Hugh Walpole), but many wrote pieces specifically for that particular Gift Book. If it was easy for prose writers to compose (and in a few cases, throw off) a paragraph or two to aid the cause, many took their responsibilities more seriously and wrote carefully judged pieces to the subject. For poets the task was harder (poems taking longer to compose) and some, again, sent in poems from their backlist. Others, like Edmund Gosse, Austin Dobson, Lewis Morris, Swinburne and John Masefield (in 1939 the Poet Laureate) devised pieces specifically for the books. For *The Queen's Book of the Red Cross* he remembered

> *. . . a moonless night in a blasted town,*
> *And the cellar-steps with their army-*
> *blanket-screen,*
> *And the stretcher-bearers, groping and*
> *stumbling down*
> *To the Red Cross struggle with Death in*
> *the ill-lit scene.*

Swinburne, who by 1905 was elderly, frail and seldom seen, struck out in that year's *Queen's Christmas Carol* with a surprisingly fierce comparison between a boy who can go 'galloping over the moorland' and another who

> *. . . with darkness and toil fast bound,*
> *Bound in misery and iron fast,*
> *Drags his nakedness underground,*
> *Sees the mine as the world at last.*

Byam Shaw's main illustration for Rider Haggard's 'Magepa the Buck' in *Princess Mary's Gift Book*

Illustrators, too, responded with differing degrees of effort. Most, it must be said, seem to have submitted existing work, but there are exceptions – from Fred Pegram, J Morton Sale, Edmund Blampied and Bip Pares, for example. R L Knowles, designer of the famous endpapers to the Everyman book series, drew the title page to *The Blinded Soldiers and Sailors Gift Book*. Rex Whistler designed endpapers for *The Princess Elizabeth Gift Book*.

Some Writers Who Contributed

Of all the writers and artists who graced the Gift Book pages, many remain familiar today. Many of course have faded. Some of the great names include:

Arnold Bennett

Being prolific, popular and well-regarded (except by Virginia Woolf) it is no surprise to find him writing for Gift Books. Much of his copious journalism has, being of its time, inevitably disappeared but his novels are still read (and televised) today. Best-known titles include *The Old Wives' Tale, The Card, Riceyman Steps,* the *Clayhanger* trilogy, *Anna of the Five Towns* and numerous Five Towns stories. Born in the Staffordshire Potteries, Bennett fictionalised them as the Five Towns (though there are actually six). Moving to London, he fictionalised himself in *A Man From The North* and he fictionalised the capital itself in various novels. Having spent some years in France, he made good the experiences in *The Old Wives' Tale, The Pretty Woman* (a 'French' tale set in London) and in his published diaries. He also wrote plays. In 1918 (for the last months of the war) he was made Director of Propaganda.

'Instructing Her Dolly in the Art of Going Off Nicely to By-Byes'
by M E Gray, in *Princess Mary's Gift Book*

Marjorie Bowen

Bowen was a writer of children's and historical novels (*Viper of Milan*, *A Sword Decides*, etc.). She is no relation to the later Elizabeth Bowen, 'Marjorie Bowen' being a pseudonym for Gabrielle Margaret Vere Campbell. Her mother, Josephine Vere Campbell, was the author of a number of Edwardian novels of domestic disturbance and infidelity. Mother and daughter did not get on, and both had marriages sufficiently unhappy and unfaithful to feed their fictional stories: Josephine was widowed and impoverished; 'Marjorie' too was widowed. She fell in love with another man but he also died; she married another but the marriage was, at best, a qualified success.   Her novels were at least as 'sensational' as her mother's had been.

Robert Bridges
As Poet Laureate (from 1913) he could hardly refuse an invitation to contribute to several Gift Books.   After several shorter volumes, his *Collected Poems* in 1912 became a commercial success, so the war saw him, one might say, at the top of his game.   In 1916 he published an inspiring *The Spirit of Man*.

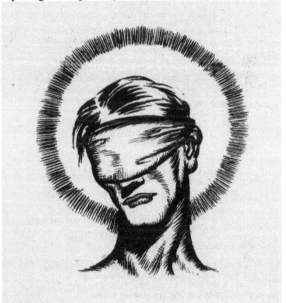

Anna Zinkeissen again, with a tailpiece in *Soho Centenary*

Hall Caine
In his day he needed no introduction.   Sir Thomas Henry Hall Caine, as he eventually became, was the son of a blacksmith, the friend and ultimately biographer of Rossetti, and an author of best-selling if risible adventure novels, frequently with a religious theme: *The Scapegoat, The Prodigal Son, The White Prophet* etc.

147

(One of his plays was deemed so offensive to Muslims that it was banned. From 1895 he was a tax exile in the Isle of Man. *Plus ça change.*) Given his enormous sales, his was a useful name for any list. Less spoken of was his marriage to the under-age Mary Chandler. (At that time, though not for much longer, the age of consent had been just thirteen.) Caine was the editor of the 1905 and 1908 *Queen Alexandra* Gift Books and of the 1914 *King Albert's Book.* (King Albert later created him an Officer of the Order of Leopold of Belgium.)

G K Chesterton

Probably the best-known, certainly one of the most prolific essayists of his day – to him, journalism was 'the easiest of professions' – a poet, critic and popular novelist, he is most famous nowadays for his Father Brown detective stories. Off-beat as those short stories were, Chesterton's novels were (deliberately) stranger. His first, *The Napoleon of Notting Hill* (1904), set the tone, casting its eye ahead to a violent and quasi-medieval London of the future. Others gave a similarly off-kilter view of the world, and allowed Chesterton to hide his pessimism behind a mask of manic invention and humour. Many of his polemical essays took the same approach, although at times he was visibly unable to hide his anger and censorious distaste for the world he saw around him.

His fierce patriotism and prolificacy may explain why he appears in half a dozen of the books discussed here, his last appearance being in *Princess Elizabeth's Gift Book* published in the year before his death.

Walter de la Mare

His first book of children's poems, *Songs of Childhood*, had been published under a pseudonym in 1902 and attracted little notice, but *Peacock Pie* had come out in

1913 to follow his successful prose story for children, *The Three Mulla-Mulgars* (1910). Yet his name was still not well known enough for him to be invited into Gift Books of the First World War. Many of the works for which he is now remembered came later, including the children's poetry anthology *Come Hither* in 1923 and his many short stories and poems across later years. His several appearances in Gift Books began after the war, in the 1920s, and continued into the Second World War.

Sir Arthur Conan Doyle

We remember him for Sherlock Holmes, but Conan Doyle dearly wished we didn't; he saw himself as a historical novelist. His first Gift Book appearance, in 1898, came when he was at the height of his Sherlock Holmes fame – though already determined to shake it off – and he continued to write for Gift Books both in the First World War and in the Twenties, when he looked back upon the war as 'the Dark Ages'. During the war he submitted a war poem and an Empire story. What he absolutely would *not* countenance for the Gift Books was any mention of the Great Detective – despite dragging him back in book form in 1917 for *His Last Bow* and – who knows how reluctantly? – in 1927 for *The Case-Book of Sherlock Holmes*.

John Galsworthy

Still famous for his *Forsyte Saga* (twice televised), though many of his other novels are worth reading, Galsworthy began his literary career as a playwright with *The Silver Box* in 1906. His plays and stories retain much of their interest because of the clear social commentary that underpins them, and his 1910 play, *Justice,* is credited with helping reform the use of solitary confinement in prisons; it is only one of several of his plays to become a major talking point in its day.

Keen as he was on social reform, he himself came from an upper middle class background (he was educated at Harrow), and his private life was frowned upon by some members of that generally hidebound social stratum. Why? Because he lived with his cousin's wife for ten years before marrying her. The fact was well known among the literary set but, as would not be the case today, remained unreported in the media. None of his novels achieved the success of the *Forsyte Saga* (initially three and finally nine novels plus some short stories), though he won a Nobel Prize for Literature in 1932. His eminent status is reflected in the five Gift Book appearances listed here, which include short stories, a snatch of biography, a poem, and the Foreword to *The Queen's Gift Book*.

Anna Zinkeissen, this time in full colour: 'Manhattan', in *Soho Centenary*

Sir Edmund Gosse

Sir Edmund lent a touch of class and erudition to three Gift Books, being a noted literary critic and essayist, and the author of a celebrated autobiographical book, *Father and Son* (1907), which is, in truth, the only one of his works much read today.

Beatrice Harraden

In the closing years of the 19th century few would have predicted that the famously tiny Miss Harraden would become sufficiently respectable to be asked to contribute to three of our Gift Books. A strong suffragist (though educated at the prestigious Cheltenham Ladies College), a feminist activist and author of numerous short stories and, for their time, adult novels, including the million-selling *Ships That Pass In The Night* (1893), she returned, latish in life, to writing children's stories. Two of them appear here, in *Princess Mary's Gift Book* and *The Queen's Gift Book*, while she presents a more patriotic tale for *The Blinded Soldiers and Sailors Gift Book*, which ends: *Eight months later Peter was killed at Ypres, one of the many thousands of heroes, unnamed in despatches, unknown, undistinguished, yet helping to make an imperishable record of our country's honour.* In 1915, when that book was published, no one knew that the Battle of Ypres (20th October to 22nd November 1914) was but the first great slaughter at Ypres. There would be two more Battles of Ypres, after which few would think it glorious to die 'unnamed in despatches, unknown, undistinguished' in the Western Front mud.

Maurice Hewlett

A fashionable name in the early 20th century (he died in 1923), well known in literary circles, and now remembered, if at all, for his historical novels and his poems. *The Forest Lovers* (1898) and *The Queen's Quair* (1904) were perhaps his most famous novels although, as the Edwardian age progressed, his novels became more concerned with political and social reform.

Rudyard Kipling
The Jungle Book (1894), *Kim* (1901), *Just So Stories* (1902), *Rewards and Fairies* (1910), the *Plain Tales From the Hills* (1888), the short stories, the *Barrack Room Ditties* (1892), the Nobel Prize in 1907... In the early 20th century, not only was Kipling one of our most famous authors but he had become synonymous with soldiers, Empire and Our Country. In Gift Books of the First World War he could not be left out – even if that war would leave him broken by his son's death, for which he blamed himself. But just as his writing embraced far more than war and Empire, so did the period of his contributions span far more than the Great War. We find Gift Book contributions from Kipling running all the way from 1898 to 1935.

Sir Henry Newbolt
Familiar to all – though less so in recent years – if only for the classroom staple, 'Drake's Drum', Newbolt's stirring and patriotic ballads are only part of what he wrote. The anthology that poem came from, *Admirals All* (1897) ran to 21 editions in its first two years. The next anthology, *The Island Race* (1898) sold almost as well. His poems ran alongside short stories, novels and a *Naval History of the War, 1914-18*. (He had been Controller of Wireless and Cables during the war.)

Owen Seaman
A man-about-town, as befits a satirist, an editor of *Punch* from 1906 to 1932 and a contributor of burlesques, parodies and light verse elsewhere, he was a man whose

success was achieved despite, one feels, the opinions of many about him: they thought him smug and right-wing – too snobbish and dictatorial to be editor of *Punch*. It is no surprise to find that most of what he wrote during the war was intensely patriotic.

A Prehistoric Humorist!

EDWARD T. REED.

OCCASIONAL CONTRIBUTORS

Leading names who appear less often than one might have thought include **H G Wells**, who wrote often and at such great length elsewhere on science, society and war. **Thomas Hardy** was included only once, and the worthy and prolific **Mrs Humphrey Ward** just twice – as was **Winston Churchill**, **Baroness Orczy** and **Hillaire Belloc**. The Bloomsbury Group and their acolytes are mainly absent, although literary lights such as **Rebecca West**, **Edmund Blunden** and **David Garnett** all submitted – as, in contrast, did **Sapper** and **Edgar Wallace**. Surprising names such as **Emmeline Pankhurst**, and the 'sensation' novelist **Mrs Braddon**, and the sexual pioneer **Edward Carpenter** all sneak into the commodious *King Albert's Book*. **J M Barrie** makes 4 appearances.

Then there are the poets. Apart from Kipling and Robert Bridges, the books present works by (among others) **Laurence Binyon**, **Aldous Huxley**, **Henry Newbolt**, **J C Squire**, **John Drinkwater**, **Gilbert Murray**, **G K Chesterton**, **Walter de la Mare**, **Humbert Wolfe**, **W H Davies**, **Edith Sitwell** and **Vita Sackville-West**. A literary coda, as it were, comes with the later Gift Books around the Second World War, when we meet contemporary authors such as **Vera Brittain**, **H E Bates**, **Eric Linklater**, **A G MacDonell**, **J B Priestley**, **Hugh Walpole**, **Noel Streatfeild** and **Peter Cheyney**.

Finally – though at the time these names were far from an afterthought – we should not forget the celebrities and the royals. Here the presence of a signature made an enormous difference. One's eyes will quickly flick past a throw-away line from somebody royal or famous, but how differently these entries seem when, immediately below, we see the signature, that person's actual handwriting in (apparently) real ink.

THE ARTISTS

'Three Kings of Orient' in *Edmund Dulac's Picture-Book*

Pictures made the Gift Books. Many buyers, indeed, might have looked only at the pictures. Certainly, when one bought a book crammed with beautiful illustrations – sometimes funny, sometimes sad, sometimes inspiring – often in full colour, one knew that, apart from having given money to a good cause, one had got a decent return for one's precious few shillings. The book buyer of today, spoilt for choice, should remember that in those days, illustrations of high quality from artists like Rackham and Dulac were normally available only in de luxe gift books that cost a great deal more. So these special books were not only for a good cause, they were democratic. They invited everyone to share.

Of the many artists and illustrators of the day, only a fraction could be selected for the Gift Books – though a few names recur. **Lewis Baumer** graced three of the books, as did Sir **Luke Fildes**, the grand old man of Victorian painting. Baumer was principally an illustrator, best at delicately-done children, flowers and maidens (often in pastel), while Sir Luke had been one of the great Victorian genre artists, whose most famous work was the 1874 *Applicants for Admission to a Casual Ward*. **Claude A Shepperson** is a name largely forgotten now, but his graceful illustrative work can be found in many magazines of the day; he was adept in black & white and in watercolour.

Inevitably, most of the artists chosen were illustrators. Best-known today is the creator of fantastical inventions, **W Heath Robinson**, who even then was the most well-known of the three Robinson brothers. He contributed several pictures, and his brother **Charles** (better known for lovely children's drawings) made one for the *Queen's Gift Book*. The two **Brock** brothers contributed – **Charles** (C E) and **Henry** (H M). They are not related to another contributor, **Sir Thomas Brock**, the sculptor who designed the final image of Queen Victoria on British coins (she had reigned so long that her image had to be updated twice) and the Queen Victoria Memorial which now stands in The Mall.

Sir W B Richmond contributed this symbolic study, *The Crown of Peace*:

Arthur Rackham and Edmund Dulac were perhaps the most desirable illustrators for any Gift Book, having illustrated several of their own, as well as many children's story books by other writers. Kay Nielsen appears, as does Hugh Thomson and Leonard Raven-Hill. His name is little known today but from the 1890s to the 1920s he was recognised as a superb – and prolific – black & white illustrator and cartoonist. (The hyphen appeared and disappeared from his name with puzzling irregularity.)

Other artists made isolated appearances, most notably in the 1924 *British Legion Album*, where we find Sir Herbert Hughes-Stanton, H M Bateman, William

Rothenstein, **John Hassall, William Orpen, Augustus John, W Heath Robinson, C R W Nevinson, Solomon J Solomon** and nautical artist **W L Wyllie**. *King Albert's Book* attracted even more leading artists, including Solomon again, **Poynter, Dicksee, Sir Luke Fildes, Richmond, Waterlow, Briton Riviere, J J Shannon, Pennell** and **Nicholson**, and the illustrators **Rackham, Dulac, Brock, Crane, Raven-Hill** and **Kay Nielsen**. **Edward Bawden** is in *The Legion Book*. Search around and you will also find **Eric Ravilious, John Sargent, Laura Knight** and **Clare Leighton**.

And Finally . . .

Scattered through the books (though not in all) are musical interludes that we should not overlook – pieces we can sit with at the piano and play at home, pieces by **Elgar**, **Ethel Smyth**, **Stanford**, **Edward German**, **Debussy** and several more.

All these names made sumptuous fare. They had all contributed their work for free, and now it was your turn to contribute to the cause – and especially in war-time, how could you refuse? Not only would you get to keep, cherish, and look again and again at a book of beauty, a panoply of delights, but you would have the satisfaction of knowing that you had thrust your hand into your pocket to help. You had responded, perhaps, to the handwritten appeal from Her Royal Highness Princess Alice, Countess of Athlone, President, Women's Section, British Legion, who hoped *that this beautiful and interesting album may find a ready sale on behalf of the most deserving cause, for which it has been compiled.*

Every little helps. One of the 38 pages of advertisements in *The British Legion Album*

About the author

James Havers was a reluctant convert to the ebook. His collection of well over three thousand ink-on-paper books is housed in a room lined with custom-built bookshelves and, in deference to the books or perhaps out of sheer cussedness, he refuses to take his e-reader into his library, keeping that room sacred to books that can be held, felt and, with some of the older volumes, smelt. (Most have been bought second-hand.) He owns copies of all the books mentioned in *Please Buy This Book* and has at least one example of all the paperbacks described in his latest book, *When A Paperback Cost Sixpence*, published by Prospero Books in late 2015.

16152660R00097

Printed in Great Britain
by Amazon